EMPATH FOR BEGINNERS

Improve Self-Esteem, Overcome Fear, Find Your Sense Of Self, Learn To Stop Absorbing Negative Energies, Increase Self-Confidence, Achieve Emotional Healing

Valery Blake

© Copyright 2020 by Valery Blake. All right reserved.

The work contained herein has been produced with the intent to provide relevant knowledge and information on the topic on the topic described in the title for entertainment purposes only. While the author has gone to every extent to furnish up to date and true information, no claims can be made as to its accuracy or validity as the author has made no claims to be an expert on this topic. Notwithstanding, the reader is asked to do their own research and consult any subject matter experts they deem necessary to ensure the quality and accuracy of the material presented herein.

This statement is legally binding as deemed by the Committee of Publishers Association and the American Bar Association for the territory of the United States. Other jurisdictions may apply their own legal statutes. Any reproduction, transmission or copying of this material contained in this work without the express written consent of the copyright holder shall be deemed as a copyright violation as per the current legislation in force on the date of publishing and subsequent time thereafter. All additional works derived from this material may be claimed by the holder of this copyright.

The data, depictions, events, descriptions and all other information forthwith are considered to be true, fair and accurate unless the work is expressly described as a work of fiction. Regardless of the nature of this work, the Publisher is exempt from any responsibility of actions taken by the reader in conjunction with this work. The Publisher acknowledges that the reader acts of their own accord and releases the author and Publisher of any responsibility for the observance of tips, advice, counsel, strategies and techniques that may be offered in this volume.

TABLE OF CONTENTS

Introduction 1
Chapter 1 *Understanding The Enigma Called An Empath* 4
Chapter 2 *It Is Not A Disease, Curse, Or A Problem* 9
Chapter 3 *It Is A Gift, But You Will Need To Learn A Lot To Harness It* 14
Chapter 4 *Possible Explanations Of Development Of Powers That Make You An Empath* 21
Chapter 5 *There Is A Difference Between Empathy And An Empath* 24
Chapter 6 *Who Is An Empath?* 28
Chapter 7 *The Struggles Of Living As An Unawakened Empath* 31
Chapter 8 *Unraveling The Nature Of An Empath* 35
Chapter 9 *What Does It Mean To Be An Empath?* 42
Chapter 10 *Do You Think You Are An Empath?* 51
Chapter 11 *All Empaths Aren't The Same- What Kind Of An Empath Are You?* 62
Chapter 12 *What Difference Does Being An Empath Have On Life?* 68
Chapter 13 70
The Thin Line Of Being An Empath 70
Chapter 14 *Beware Of The Things That Can Take You Down* 71
Chapter 15 *Learning To Be An Empath With Confidence* 76
Conclusion 79
Description 80

INTRODUCTION

Being an empath can be an overwhelming experience. An empath can be living a miserable life feeling the pain and agony without having any knowledge of it in real life. It usually makes things very complicated and challenging for the empath. Yet, openly talking about it or an attempt to explain it to others often results in ridicule. It can only mean one thing; in most cases than not, an empath is forced to live with the circumstances without a way out.

This book will help you in understanding the core issues and also the possible ways to deal with them. I congratulate you on purchasing this book, and thank you for doing so. In this book, I will try to explain what it means to be an empath and what an empath usually feels and goes through.

This book will try to help you understand the primary challenges in front of empaths and effective ways to deal with them.

Being an empath is not a curse as most people believe, and also not some powerful boon that popular literature tries to project. An empath isn't some sort of a mutant. This book will help you understand the realistic aspect of being an empath and how to deal with it in real life.

We will dig deep and understand what it means to be an empath and the impact it can have on life. There is a lot of confusion surrounding empaths. This book will try to explain that in detail so that you have better clarity on the subject.

It will explain the things that negatively influence the lives of empaths and also the attributes that will help them grow stronger.

This book will dwell upon the subject and explain what it means and who needs healing.

It will explain ways to enhance your abilities and ward off negative influences.

This book will deal with the concept of empath healing and how it can work for you. It would help you in overcoming your anxieties and keeping negative influences away while you try to find joy in life.

This book will try to debunk the myths most beginners have about empath healing and will set a clear and defined path so that you can develop a clear understanding of the subject.

This book is straightforward and easy to understand so that everyone can take advantage of this information.

I hope that you will be able to get the full advantage of this book.

There are plenty of books on this subject on the market; thanks again for choosing this one! Every effort has been made to ensure it is full of as much useful information as possible; please enjoy it!

PART I
BEING AN EMPATH

CHAPTER 1
Understanding The Enigma Called An Empath

Being an Empath is Normal

Our world has a high affinity for things being normal. It has rigid notions about all things being rational and standard, and anything that doesn't conform to those standards is abnormal.

- On meeting others, it is a norm to strike a conversation. People not trying to do that can be termed as abnormal or socially awkward.
- Our kind has always felt more secure in groups. People feeling insecure or uncomfortable in groups can also be termed as abnormal or awkward.
- We like to be in crowds, pretend to enjoy the company of others, but hide our genuine emotions or current emotional state. Yet strangely, if someone can sense those emotions or feels them, we begin feeling threatened or vulnerable. We may also call such a person abnormal.

Abnormal is a term the world has devised to brand anything that is beyond the average reach or common comprehension. It is the bracket in which empaths generally fall.

Being an empath is not abnormal. An empath is also like being any other person in the world. It is just that an empath has some additional powers than others, and sometimes even that individual fails to understand and appreciate those powers and abilities.

Who Is an Empath?

You are an empath if you have the superhuman ability to understand and absorb the mental or emotional state of others near you. Here, you would need to follow caution in comprehending the term carefully. Most people may be able to make an informed guess about someone else's mental or emotional state. Some people may even be able to address them emphatically. However, very few people with a special gift of deep sensitivity will be able to feel that mental or emotional state within themselves. Such people are empaths. Such people not only understand the pain others are feeling but also sense that pain deep within themselves.

A person can learn to be emphatic so that he/she can have better connections with others. An empath will be born with the sensitivities that help him/her in feeling the pain, emotions, and discomfort felt or experienced by others.

Being an empath can be a roller-coaster ride. An empath will feel people around, and their emotions will have a profound impact on him/her. These can be overwhelming experiences for an empath, and they can make an empath naturally shy of crowds or public exposure. An empath with poor control over the gift may find it increasingly challenging to be in large groups as the energies around the empath will be affecting him/her continuously, even without talking to the people with such powers.

Empaths are highly sensitive people. They can feel pain, emotions, energies of people around them far more intensely. However, the problem doesn't end just there. Some empaths with powerful sensitivities, and very porous boundaries can not only feel them but also begin absorbing them. It can become a challenge as they become a storehouse of all the negative energy, pain, and stress around them.

Hence, an empath can be an individual with a superhuman ability to look deep inside the heart and mind of a person in front beyond the surface level façade. Such empaths can play a significant role in helping others as they are gifted healers.

However, an empath can also be a person who is unable to control the amount of negative energy seeping in and hence forced to live in constant pain and discomfort.

These are just the two sides of being an empath. On the contrary to what most people think, being an empath is neither a curse nor a boon; it is merely a state of heightened sensitivities and the amount of command and understanding an individual has over them.

Some empaths may have comparatively low sensitivities and may not get affected too much. Whereas others can have relatively much higher sensitivities, and they may keep feeling overwhelmed most of the time if they have not strengthened personal boundaries.

Irrespective of the level of sensitivities you have, being an empath is not a curse. If you have not yet mastered control over your sensibilities, you may feel overwhelmed with negative energies, thoughts, and feelings. It isn't even very uncommon to have a strong aversion to crowded places. It is all very much possible and common. However, this is not how it has to be forever.

An empath can quickly learn to use this gift of heightened sensitivities to read people around and have a deep insight into the human psyche.

Some of the most potent characteristics that may make the life of an empath difficult. However, an empath can easily handle it if he/she learns to manage the powers properly.

An empath is neither a maniac nor a wizard. An empath is also just like everyone else, a great human being with some gifts that the empath can sharpen and use as tools for healing others. However, if the empath chooses to ignore them, they can turn into thorns that may start creating a lot of nuisance within.

Boons and Banes of an Empath

Character traits of an empath can be many, and I have not taken the best of those here because most empaths may not have all of them in common. These are the four traits that are usually common in most empaths and need to be understood carefully, or else they can turn even against them.

Intuitive

It is the most common and most understandable trait in empaths. Everyone has some degree of intuition. The gut feeling within us warns us of dangers and guides us away from them. This feeling is the best answer in most circumstances for us. However, empaths have a special gift of intuition. They are highly sensitive beings with the ability to listen to their inner thoughts when it comes to judging others carefully. It is effortless for them to distinguish between positive and negative energies in others as they can feel them directly.

The events in the future are a direct result of the actions in the present, and the intuitiveness of any individual can help in determining it. Because empaths have a clear edge in this area, they are better at guessing future events.

However, even this outstanding power can work against empaths if they do not exercise proper control of their capabilities and emotions. Empaths are highly sensitive beings, and they can quickly get motivated to cut themselves off from others to block the inflow of negative energies that can help them in being intuitive.

Some empaths may also begin relying on other inputs like their dreams, telepathic contributions, precognitive abilities, and sensations around them, and this can also increase their intuitive powers.

All these are powers that empaths can utilize if they have realized their gift. Not all empaths will be able to recognize all the abilities, and some may not be able to achieve any of these, yet they have a world of opportunities open in front of them to utilize.

Realizing the power of intuition comes quickly to an empath because the sensitivities are very high. However, it is a gift that needs to be harnessed through practice and focus on gut feelings. It is also the gift that will help an empath in forging strong relationships.

Most empaths are vulnerable to energy vampires that can drain them of all the emotional energy and leave them feeling exhausted. The toxic behavior of people around you can begin stressing them physically, mentally, and emotionally.

The power of intuition can help an empath in avoiding such people and situations. However, all empaths may not have the power of intuition developed in the same manner. But, empaths can augment this power nonetheless, and being an empath always helps.

Intense

Being an empath doesn't come without some riders, and being intense is one among them. An empath is an individual who feels things far more strongly than others. It means that something that may not even lead to a passing thought in the mind of a person may shake an empath deeply. For instance, we oversee many unfortunate people and beings while passing on a road. Most people don't even bat an eyelid as they are busy with their lives. However, that may not turn out to be the case with an empath. An empath may feel deeply saddened by the sight or mere presence of such people around. If helping such people is not possible, the pain and hurt may stay deep inside the heart of an empath.

In the same way, an empath may also feel other emotions like love and trust profoundly and may get hurt more thoroughly than others.

Uncentered

It is another battle that an empath may have to fight all life. An empath may not be able to feel at home most of the time. There is always a feeling somewhere at the back of the mind that something is out of place or something isn't right.

This anxiety comes out of the perpetual outside energy influence an empath keeps getting that leaves that unsettling feeling.

It is not a quality or gift or even a curse; it is just a trait that empaths usually exhibit.

Perplexed

For an unawakened empath, it is not uncommon to feel perplexed most of the time. Empaths have to live in the constant agony of feeling everything wanted or unwanted around them. They experience the emotions of others around them and remain filled with pain and anguish. They have weak personal boundaries, and hence separating feelings of others, and the self keeps on becoming increasingly difficult for them. Either it is the painful exposure to large crowds or the guilty pleasure of having seclusion, unawakened empaths have a hard time either way. A struggle between pain and guilt is always going on.

However, that's not an experience for every empath. An awakened empath knows the art of regulating their emotions. They have firm personal boundaries that allow them to experience the feelings of others without getting lost in them.

An awakened empath would know the art of not getting lost in the problem while trying to solve it. It isn't an ability that one is born with by default. It is something that an empath needs to learn and practice.

Usually, people have absurd ideas about empaths. Most of their knowledge comes from exaggerated fiction portrayed on the idiot box and leisure literature.

Empaths are not a distinct breed or mutants with some elaborate powers. A very high number of individuals are born with above-average sensitivity. They feel emotions with higher intensity than others.

It is a fact that empaths have a heightened sense of perception and intuition, but that doesn't make them fortune-tellers. Every coin has two sides, and being an empath is no exception.

An unawakened empath with weak boundaries may live a life of suffering and pain. There is no respite for such empaths as they may feel lost all the time. Their power of discernment between their own emotions and emotions perceived by others may become weak. They may not have any respite from the constant bombardment of emotions that they do not understand, and it will take a toll on their emotional, mental, as well as physical health.

Therefore, contrary to popular beliefs, being an empath is not a bed of roses. It is just a weak and troubled mental and emotional state for the empath.

However, all that can change for an awakened empath who has control over his/her senses. A confident and awakened empath may not have the ability to predict the future or read the minds of people around him. Still, they will have the ability to assess people correctly based on the first impression left by them.

A well-functioning empath will also have the power of intuition and hence would have a better grip over things.

Therefore, being an empath is neither a bed of roses or a spikey seat. It is an ability with which you are born. It isn't something that'd go with time, and hence ignoring it won't help. If you keep forgetting it for long enough, it may fill you with anxiety, distrust, anguish, pain, and disharmony. However, if you work upon your gift, you may not only be able to get hold of your senses but also help others around you.

This book would help you in understanding what an empath means and the way to carry out empath healing so that one can stay on the right path.

CHAPTER 2
It Is Not A Disease, Curse, Or A Problem

Being an Empath- Boon or Bane?

It is not uncommon for humankind, in general, to fear and blame things, it has difficulty in understanding. Empaths need not be an exception. Even as a child, when an individual begins to show traits of an empath like:-

- Overly sensitive or shy nature
- Frequent bouts of anxiety or getting overwhelmed
- Inability to tolerate shouting or arguments
- Anxiety in crowds
- Inability to correctly fit in the mix
- Desire to remain socially isolated
- A tendency to absorb pain, stress, emotions, and symptoms of other people around

But, an Empath

- Finds it easy to assess the nature of others
- Has accurate gut feeling most of the time
- Begins predicting many events, yet to occur, with accuracy
- Develops a unique and more accurate understanding of people
- Feels the pain and sorrow of others in a real sense and can heal them better

It is common for people, including even that individual, to look for faults and problems.
As an empath, a person may:

Experience Increased Sensitivity to Light, Sound, Smell, Taste, Touch, and Temperature: This is among the first experiences an empath may have. Even as a newborn, empaths may exhibit high sensitivity to bright lights, loud noises, exotic smells, and other sensory stimuli. Such stimuli can be painful, startling, frightening, or shocking. Not only that, but it also isn't necessary for two empaths to get agitated by the same stimuli.

Begin Absorbing Stress, Emotions, and Negativity of Others: This is a common trait of empaths. They can begin absorbing the stress, emotions, and negative energies emitted by people around them. Unawakened empaths have no barriers, and hence they can't control what they consume. They are very porous, and anything and everything around them begins affecting them.

Prone to Stimulation: Empaths can begin feeling overstimulated quickly. The things that may not stimulate ordinary people easily, an empath may feel highly agitated. They may start feeling exhausted and need more alone time to replenish their energy.

Feel Things More Intensely Than Others: Empaths are sensitive. They get affected by visuals and emotions that aren't even happening in real-time. For instance, if they are only watching something graphic full of violence or sorrow, they can feel the same within themselves. They don't have filters to keep such emotions out.

Experience Emotional Burnout: They are always ready to listen to others. If the stories they hear have emotions, grief, and pain, they begin affecting them with the same intensity. It can also start causing overexertion. Every empath needs to learn to build boundaries and respect them, which most don't, becoming the cause of the trouble.

Feel Lonely and Isolated: Being an empath is maintaining a tricky balance. You open up a tad bit more, and you'll expose your boundaries and begin getting bombarded by emotions, you tighten the latch, and you'd become private. The need to have some respite usually wins, and people tend to prefer more and more seclusion leading to loneliness and social isolation. The real trick is to open up the gates but to enforce more definite boundaries, and then only an empath can have a social presence along with the peace of mind.

As you can imagine, most empaths struggle all their lives to find that balance or peace of mind because the personal space of an empath keeps getting bombarded by emotions.

Suffering and pain become part and parcel of an empath's life and finds it difficult to come to terms with the reality of creating boundaries and personal space.

Loneliness, depression, pain, overwhelming emotions, emotional confusion, and distress become a regular feature in the life of such empaths. They keep getting dragged by these and find it very hard to carry the burden of all these things.

Having a heightened sense of perceptions, intuition, and precognition can begin looking like a curse if you do not have an understanding of your gifts or know the art to utilize them. **Imagine a bird having acrophobia *(Fear of Height)*.**

Have you heard of the 'Midas Touch'? Midas had the power to turn anything into gold by a simple touch. It was a boon. Yet, it became a bane because it starved him. Even the food touched by him turned into gold.

Empaths have a heightened perception of pain, suffering, and emotions of others. As long as they can enforce boundaries around them to prevent illness, suffering, and feelings of others from permeating into them, they will be able to help others and live a fruitful life. The problem begins when empaths fail to have such boundaries, and they start acting like a blotting paper soaking up all the pain and suffering around them.

Being an empath is not a problem. The inability to have sufficient control over your power, condition, or traits is the cause of the malice that empaths face.

Being an empath is not a disease, a curse, or a problem.

It is a gift you need to encash. Recognizing and realizing this gift is a must. Once you recognize this gift, you'll know the number of lives you can touch with your abilities.

There Can Be Challenges, But You Aren't Crazy

In the beginning, unawakened empaths fail to understand that the confusion, delusion, and a series of emotions unrelated to their personal experiences are just a part of being an empath.

All empaths are highly sensitive people. It merely means that they can feel the emotions and energies around them more profoundly than others. Not only the powers of people around them, but some may also be able to handle the vibrancy radiated from the plants and animals.

Generally, unawakened empaths aren't able to differentiate between the emotions originating within them and the pain, suffering, and emotions absorbed from the environment, and this can leave them perplexed. The thought that they might be crazy or abnormal may easily cross their mind several times.

The higher the number of recurrences of such instances, the more cemented the belief that they might be crazy gets.

Biggest Misconception to Be Cleared

The mental troubles, emotional burdens, unhappiness, and delusions are not because they are empaths. It is there because they haven't done anything to strengthen their defenses. Unawakened empaths are usually porous, and hence there is nothing to stop the feelings and emotions of others from affecting them.

Being an empath makes you capable in one direction. You get an advantage in something. However, every new power comes with a cost. Being an empath makes you capable of feeling emotions and energies with higher sensitivity that others can't. But that comes with a price. You open up to a whole lot of emotions and energies around you.

You'd need to learn to be selective. You can't let this be overused.

Consider your hypersensitivities to be a battery-operated accessory. If you keep it powered on all the time, even though it may not be performing any useful function, it'd be using up the battery. Because the accessory would be on and geared up, it'd also keep getting entangled here and there, adding to the trouble.

Therefore, you'll see that keeping it powered on all the time is not only inefficient and energy-draining but also an added pain.

The same is the case with empaths and the extra-sensory powers they possess.

An empath can have hypersensitivities in a wide range of areas. An empath may also attract negative energies and have weak boundaries. Getting influenced by them would become easy. You will have very little control over them.

These will keep posing challenges in front of an empath. The important thing is to realize that you aren't crazy, and there is a way to get control of the situation, and it isn't challenging.

Public Ridicule, Unanswered Questions, and Constant Tussles Can be Addressed

Public Ridicule

It can be challenging for the uninitiated to understand the qualities an empath may possess. It may lead to public ridicule. However, public ridicule over your abilities, sensitivities, and behavior must be your last concern as society in general never understands people who don't fall in their standard. It has always ridiculed, mocked, and outcast people it didn't understand. Most renowned scientists, reformers, and harbingers of social change have had to face that, and hence that is something that must not concern you.

When the society ridicules, it merely means either you are doing something wrong that doesn't conform to its standards, or you are doing something it doesn't understand. As long as you aren't doing something illegal, you do not need to worry.

Unanswered Questions

It is natural for an empath to have a lot of unanswered questions. There can be a lot that an empath may not understand. There are no exact answers to 'why,' but there are answers to 'what now.'

An empath may have a lot of questions.
- Why do they feel the way they do?
- Why do they feel so drained in the company of others?
- Why is their power of intuition better than others?
- Why do they feel so overwhelmed in public places?
- Why are they so emotional?
- Why are they always so inclined to help others?
- Why is it so hard for them to say no and avoid toxic people?
- Why do they even feel emotions utterly unrelated to their experiences?
- What is the reason for scattered thoughts and the mind-fog they experience?

These are just some of the questions. The list can be endless, as every empath can have completely different struggles and experiences.

However, the answer to all the mental clutter lies in understanding your abilities and reinforcing your boundaries.

Empaths are prone to get influenced by the external energies as they are very porous. But, that doesn't always have to be the case always. You can still learn to strengthen personal defenses and only allow emotions and energies with the private sphere selectively. It is possible to master it, and you can easily do it with practice.

Constant Tussles

An empath may feel constant trouble all the time as the mind and heart may not agree on the same things. There will be times when your intuition will be telling you to do something while common sense may be directing you in a completely different direction. All this is not only possible but also highly probable.

Most empaths have an intuitive power that's reliable, and that may make them sense danger or sticky situations even when it isn't visible through logic. Also, most of the time, empaths will be able to form a very accurate description of a person meeting for the first time based on the first impression. It is besides the fact that most people try to hide their true nature in the first meeting and seek to be at their best behavior. However, hiding true self from empaths can be difficult as they can sense the energies and vibes more accurately.

However, gut feelings and vibes do not conform to popular logic, and this may lead to constant tussles. They may find it hard to determine what to do and what to put aside.

You must understand that these are minor struggles that an empath undergoes. An empath can easily overcome these struggles by following the gift and learning to harness that gift.

An awakened empath will be in a much better position to use the powers effectively and conduct life without dilemmas. The answers to complicated questions would come quickly, and without a doubt and trusting the gut feeling would become much more comfortable for an empath.

It is essential that you clearly understand that being an empath is not a disease or a curse. It is an unrealized boon. You can learn to harness this energy to lead a perfectly balanced life and also have some additional powers to help others whom no one understands.

CHAPTER 3
It Is A Gift, But You Will Need To Learn A Lot To Harness It

Discovering and Appreciating the Gift and Seeking Answers

Being an empath is not a choice we make. It is something most empaths are born with or develop these sensitivities in exceptional circumstances like accidents, violent encounters, and other such traumatic events.

Initially, it can be reasonable to be confused about the powers and various sensations that may come along, as all of them may be unpleasant. However, it is prudent to adapt to the changes you are experiencing and discover your gift.

Living with these powers is like getting trapped in a room with a ferocious dog. Either you'll learn to tame that dog and make it act upon your instructions, or that dog will make your life difficult with constant growling, threatening, and attacks.

The realization of your powers is the first step towards real emancipation. You must realize that these are powers, and they can help you in helping others as well as yourself.

An empath is a person who can feel the pain and emotions of others more deeply. However, just sensing the problem is not going to help anyone. It is only going to propagate that pain at one other place, i.e., in your heart. If you realize your gift, you'll be able to address the issue specifically and help yourself and others.

Doing that is not very difficult, contrary to what most people believe. It is a gift that's inside you, and you only need to realize it. Some simple efforts can help you in achieving your abilities quickly and make you feel that being an empath is not a bane but a boon.

However, that's not going to happen until you acknowledge, accept, and appreciate your gift.

If you want to own your gift in the real sense, you must:

Acknowledge the Gift: If you are an empath, feeling for others will be your second nature. The harder you try to fight it, the more difficult it'll get for you. It is a gift that you possess, and you must acknowledge and appreciate it.

There will be times when people would find it easy to overlook someone in distress and pretend as if nothing is happening. There is no need for you to imitate as if you also belong in that group.

As an empath, feeling the pain of others would be your second nature. You'd be able to sense a lot of things that others won't, and there is no need to be embarrassed about them. There is no measure for that.

You must acknowledge that you feel that you feel differently than others. Your senses are more durable and more powerful. You may not only be able to feel the pain and emotion visible in front but may also be able to handle the energies around you.

Do Not Undermine Your Gut Feeling: Our gut feeling is an exceptional phenomenon. It can help us make strange decisions. Most people have a gut feeling fuelled by the stress hormones and lead to a fight or flight response. For them, the gut feeling is just an escape mechanism devised just to escape uncomfortable scenarios.

However, gut feeling or intuition can be a very distinct phenomenon for empaths. They have very high sensitivities, and their instinct is mostly a sum of those sensitivities. As an empath, if you are sensing danger at someplace, it is better to trust your gut feeling than to take chances as the likeliness of your intuition turning out to be true is very high.

While intuition is an escape mechanism in most people, for an empath, it can be a survival mechanism.

Setting Boundaries: Weak personal boundaries are among the most significant cause of concern for empaths. You can term empaths to be friendly people who can get affected by the pain of others. They do not need the spoken word for feeling the pain of others. They may act as magnets for such pain and suffering. Their energy fields are constantly scanning for people in pain and may be able to feel the pain of others in the vicinity. It can be a big challenge, and there is no way a person will be able to help all, and hence the life of an empath can become an unending saga of pain.

It is not unnatural for people to recognize such empaths and then begin exploiting the weakness about helping others. Such clingy people can also become energy vampires that may become very demanding and draining. The only way out of this problem is to have firm personal boundaries. Empaths would have to train themselves to recognize such energy vampires. It is something that may take time, but they'll be able to identify those people that are a constant energy drain.

They'll also have to strengthen their energy fields so that they do not keep getting bombarded with unsolicited emotions. They'll have to learn the art of managing their energy field more strongly.

Learn to Push Away Negative Energy: It is easier said than done to propel negative energy and influences. Most people feel the vibes and energy fields emitted by others. Even in your first meeting, most people can form liking or dislike about anyone, and most likely, it stays with them. It is also true for everyone in general. Now think of an empath who has a distinct ability to feel the energy vibes far more intensely.

They will be able to feel the vibes and would keep reacting to them latently, and that would also cause a lot of energy drain. It can become a big problem if there are such toxic people at the work-place or in the neighborhood. That can make the life of an empath very difficult. The easy way out for an empath is to learn to find ways to absorb or push away negative energies. There are several natural energy modulators like crystals, beautiful artifacts, and plants that can help in absorbing negative energies around you, and you'll be able to work far more peacefully.

Shun the Feeling of Victimhood: The need for love, admiration, and adoration is always there in most of us. It is natural for someone with intense feelings to have these needs even more. The fact that they feel more strongly for others and can feel the emotions better makes them long even more for the love and devotion of others.

However, empaths are complicated. They are not superficial. It can be challenging for others to understand them and have a fine-tuning with them, and this can leave them longing for love, admiration, and appreciation.

An empath may have to learn to find love differently without losing self-worth in front of others. Realization of true self-worth is essential for empaths without being proud or boastful about it if they want to find true love and objective in their lives.

Learn to love Yourself: This is one of the most critical lessons for an empath. You must learn to love yourself. There should be no room for self-pity. You must understand that until you love and learn to appreciate yourself, your energy fields would remain weak, and you'll keep feeling vulnerable.

You Must Learn to Take Out Exhaustion and Bring Relief

It is a fact that you'll realize very soon. Empaths may begin feeling exhausted very soon. It is natural for them to feel so. Allowing so many emotions to pass over you and maintaining composure can be very taxing.

Therefore,

An Empath Must Set a Regular Sleep-Wake Cycle

Being an empath can be an everyday struggle. It isn't something that you can stop doing. An empath can begin feeling overwhelmed even by watching something on the TV or a news item. Hence, avoiding such stimuli or cutting yourself from the outside world to relax is not a practical solution.

Most people talk of a digital detox these days as there is very high information overload taking place from digital media, and escaping it is next to impossible. We are on the internet for our work, needs, and leisure all the time. It means our exposure to information coming from the internet is also very high.

Knowingly or unknowingly, this information keeps piling up and has an impact on our overall functioning ability. Typically, people can function with it, but things can be stressful with an empath as information gets processed differently in their minds. They are far more sensitive, and it may weigh them down.

Empaths must set a regular sleep-wake cycle to maintain high functionality so that their body and mind can get the needed rest.

Take Regular Breaks

Nothing can be more refreshing than regular breaks for an empath. Empaths experience emotions, feelings, and grief more intensely. Either it is a meeting or any work, they remain immersed with complete attention, and that can become very taxing.

Regular breaks can help an empath in re-energizing himself/herself and work better.

These breaks don't need to be longer, but they need to be more frequent. Even a little bit of distraction from the intense environment can help an empath in winding down and regaining the energy to function optimally. Therefore, you must keep taking short breaks as often as possible.

Deep-Breathing Exercise

It is the most important advice of the three. Deep breathing is the best tool an empath has to gather awareness and focus.

It is usual for an empath to keep getting bombarded with emotions, feelings, grief, joy, and a plethora of such emotions. They can be disturbing and distracting. They may take away focus from the main objective or even cause disorientation.

It is also easy for an empath to begin feeling agitated, flushed, sad, and disoriented. Managing all these emotions when they come without proper context can be difficult. The best way to manage them is to practice deep breathing.

Deep breathing is a simple practice that can help an empath gather awareness and bring it back to reality.

The human mind is very volatile and gets distracted easily. It can begin producing thoughts that can be even more distracting and disorienting. The best way to deal with such situations and to keep them at bay is to breathe deeply.

Whenever you begin feeling agitated or have thoughts that are causing distraction or discomfort, you can do the following:

If, it is possible, find a place to sit down comfortably
If you are standing, find a place to support your body
Keep your spine erect
Please keep your neck straight
Your shoulders should be straight but not stiff
Now, if possible, please close your eyes
For a minute, feel the silence
Please try to gather all your thoughts

There is no need to control anything
Don't try to control your thoughts
Don't try to control your breathing
Simply, become aware of your thoughts
(Pause)
Imagine it is a peaceful time now
Even a minute of silence can be of great help
Now, please bring your awareness to your breathing
Simply observe your breathing process with your awareness
No need to control your breathing yet
There is no need to do anything
Just try to become aware of your surrounding
Try to feel with all your senses
Try to hear the faintest noises in your surrounding
Please focus on any kind of noise you can hear
Even if noise is coming from the fan or the air conditioning in the room
Try to notice any other noise in the surrounding
(Long pause)
Try to feel with your body
Observe the sensation of clothes touching your skin
The sensation air creates when it touches the skin
Any other kind of sensation that you might be able to feel
(Long pause)
Now, try to smell
Try to observe the fragrance in the air
Any kind of essence that you might feel
(Long pause)
With your eyes closed
Through your awareness
Silently observe the way you breathe
At this moment, you do not need to control your breathing
Jut observe the process of breathing
Breathe in
Breathe out
Breathe in
Breathe out
Breathe in
Breathe out
Your focus may waver
You may start getting thoughts
That's alright!
There is no need to bother
Simply bring your awareness back to the process of breathing
Breathe in
Breathe out

Breathe in
Breathe out
Breathe in
Breathe out
Now, we will practice deep breathing
In this process, we will slowly take deep breaths to the count of 5
Then, hold your breath to the count of 5
And, release the breath even slower to the count of 7
It will calm the mind and drive all the negative thoughts away
Through this whole process
Please keep your awareness focused on the process of breathing
If your consciousness wanders, simply bring it back
Now, very slowly and steadily start breathing in
1.....2.......3.........4...........5
Very good!
Now, hold this breath
1.....2.......3.........4...........5
Better!
Now, exhale even slower
1.....2.......3.........4...........5............6.................7
Excellent!
The process of deep breathing calms the mind
It takes away all the thoughts
The mind becomes focused on the most crucial activity for life
Breathing
Breathe in
Breathe out
Breathe in
Breathe out
Breathe in
Breathe out
Again,
Take a deep breath in through your nostrils
1... Draw your breath slowly
2..... There is no rush
3....... Feel the breath coming in
4. .... Observe the sensation it creates at the point of entry
5............ Try to feel whether the air is hot or cold
Now, hold this breath for a few seconds
1.... Let the air seep deep inside your body
2.......Let it oxygenate your blood
3.........You might feel some pressure
4...........Do not be alarmed, this pressure is good
5............ Let this air reach every cell in your body
Now, breathe out through your mouth

1.... Let the air go out slowly
2...... Do not rush
3.........Let all your worries and anxieties go out with this spent air
4............Clear your body of all the negative energy
5................ Make way for positivity
6..................Push out all the pessimism
7.......................Clear out all the air
Now, relax
Enjoy the relaxing experience of deep breathing
(Long Pause)
Breathe In
Breathe Out
Breathe In
Breathe Out
Breathe In
Breathe Out
Bring your awareness back to your surrounding
Without opening your eyes
Try to feel through all your senses
Keep breathing normally
Allow your breathing to become rhythmic
Now, you can gently open your eyes

Deep breathing is a very relaxing practice. You can perform it anywhere and make it as long or short as you want. The primary purpose of the in-depth breathing process is to bring all your senses back to you and focus them inwards and not outwards.

Deep breathing helps in bringing your wandering awareness back to you, and you'll be able to administer better control over your emotions and behavior.

If you are feeling overwhelmed or agitated, deep breathing can be immensely helpful, and it can make you feel relaxed.

CHAPTER 4
Possible Explanations Of Development Of Powers That Make You An Empath

An empath is an enigma. There is no clear explanation of why an empath must behave in the way he/she behaves. Most people believe it has something to do with our neurons, and our understanding of them is already minimal.

Others believe that the strong reception of emotions may be a result of some electromagnetic waves working vigorously in empaths. At the same time, some also think that it can be the work of some 'enthusiastic contagion.'

Several hypotheses try to explain the reason why some individuals can feel the emotions of others so strongly. However, all these are still hypotheses, and there is no actual knowledge about the exact cause.

It makes one thing clear, and that is the need to learn to live with it. There is no way you are going to be able to shake it off, and hence the faster you learn to live with it, the better.

Although an unawakened empath may feel overwhelmed, once a person learns to deal with this gift, things become comparatively easy. I have still used the expression relatively easy and not fantastic because you must not forget that an empath may have to go through a storm of emotions daily despite having all the control, command, and boundaries. Some feelings can be overwhelming even for the most experienced and awakened empaths.

However, every gift comes with some riders, and having to feel what others can't is the rider that comes with the advantage of being able to sense better than others.

Possible Scientific Explanations of the Way an Empath Feels

The Mirror Neuron System
Scientists have identified synapses that propagate empathy. It means that the people in whom those synapses are present in large numbers will be able to feel the pain experienced by others better than the ones who don't have them. These synapses act as reflective mirrors of the feelings of dread, torment, agony, and satisfaction.

Scientists believe that individuals that have a large number of such mirror neurons will be able to feel the pain, agony, and emotions of others deeply. Studies have also suggested that empaths have these mirror neurons in large quantities, and hence they are capable of more profound empathy.

Although the explanation is very close to being perfect, there is little explanation of the fact why empaths can feel emotions when they do not have direct exposure to them. It means that an empath can also begin feeling the pain and agony of a person who is nearby but not directly exposed to the empath.

Then there are several types of empaths with their distinct qualities, and explanation of all kinds is not present.

Although the mirror neuron theory only partially explains the transmitting of emotions from one person to another, it is still among the best explanations.

Electromagnetic Field

Some experts also believe that the heart and mind transmit electromagnetic waves that can lead to the spread of emotions and feelings from one person to an empath. It is a theory that fits the receiver-transmitter explanation in which everyone else is a transmitter, and the empath is a receiver. An empath can catch the bandwidth and feel those emotions.

Enthusiastic Contagion

It is another theory that tries to explain the phenomenon. It propagates an idea that states that most people release feelings of pain, excitement, joy, sorrow. The people around can catch these feelings at different levels and react accordingly.

Some people get affected by the virus of these feelings and begin reacting similarly, and that's why some news items genuinely fill a few individuals with excitement. In contrast, others may not respond that way.

It is like in a similar situation of panic; some people may begin to run and trample others while some may maintain calm and try to analyze the situation. It also doesn't explain the reason why people would give a similar reaction if they hear that news piece on the phone or they get to listen to it from other sources because, in that case, there would be no active reaction spread.

All these are theories that try to explain the phenomenon experienced by empaths. As you can see, science is still doing the guesswork, and that's why traditional medication is not very helpful in addressing the problems faced by empaths.

If an empath is suffering from excessive emotional overload or unable to control the surge of pain and emotions, the way out is through understanding the issue and finding practical solutions.

PART II
UNDERSTANDING WHAT IT MEANS TO BE AN EMPATH

CHAPTER 5
There Is A Difference Between Empathy And An Empath

The word 'empath' has a lot of mystical aura around it. The portrayal of empath characters in popular series has also not only given air to the mysticism but also popularized empaths a lot. Although this fame has drawn the attention of ordinary people towards empaths, sadly, there is also a lot of misinformation. Most of the information is beyond reality at best, making people think of empaths differently.

The simple truth is that empaths are neither magicians, mutants, not psychics. Empaths have special powers to feel energies and emotions around them more profoundly. You could sum the basics of the ability to that.

Accentuated Abilities

Some people are born with hawk eyes and can see much better than others. Others can listen better and more sharply. Some people are natural-born swimmers, while others are born runners. In the same way, while all of us have the power of intuition and the ability to sense energy and feel positive or negative vibes, some are born with the talent to detect them more intensely. Such people are called empaths.

Empaths are not abnormal people. They are also ordinary people with extraordinary power to sense the feelings of others deeply.

Peculiar Struggles

The struggles of empaths can be very different from others around them. Empaths not only feel the energies around them more profoundly, but they also act like sponges when it comes to feelings and emotions of others around them. Now, as you may know, this world is full of pain, suffering, and miseries. Absorbing feelings and emotions from the environment can quickly turn into a curse for an empath.

Most unawakened empaths who do not have substantial barriers around them or haven't trained themselves can keep absorbing such feelings and emotions, and this can make their lives very difficult. The simple act of watching TV or witnessing something painful that's not even happening in front of them in real-time can also fill them with grief. If you look around, you'll realize how difficult life can be for an empath in such circumstances.

The Difference Between Empathy and Empaths

Now, most people think that they can read and understand what others feel, and that doesn't sound that bad. The ability to understand what others are feeling and bringing yourself to that level of emotion is called empathy. It is an act of kindness. Your heart weeps for the pain suffered by others.

However, for an empath, it isn't a simple act of kindness but a natural and uncontrolled reaction. An empath will be able to feel that pain and suffering of the same intensity without having the backing of the experience bringing that reaction. Hence, most of the time, it can be confusing and complicated.

Empathy is a general human trait that makes us more humane. It helps us become kind and compassionate. However, most of the time, such compassion is superficial, and people can shrug off the feeling as soon as they leave the scene.

It isn't as simple and easy for empaths. The pain and emotions felt by them are of the same intensity, and they stay with empaths. Shrugging them off or mere pretending isn't possible for them.

Living like an empath isn't easy. An empath constantly gets bombarded by unsolicited emotions. One doesn't choose to be an empath. It gets passed on from one generation to another.

If an empath doesn't learn to cope with the emotions and works channelizing the energy properly, life can become increasingly confusing with time.

The Biggest Problem

The biggest problem that most empaths feel is that they are not able to differentiate whether the emotion they are feeling is their own or of someone else. The identification is missing, and that can make their lives miserable.

They always remain in a fix and are never able to determine the difference. It isn't just a problem for themselves but also a problem for others.

Suppose you get the power to feel the hunger of others and also have the capacity to feed. However, you are unable to identify whether it is you who is feeling hungry or someone else is hungry.

Every time that feeling of hunger strikes you, then chances are, you'll end up eating without the need of food. While this will make you overweight, others would still starve.

Weak identification can become a cause of the big problem, and it can quickly happen with empaths who don't realize their gift.

Most empaths never realize their gift and end up leading a miserable life. A power that could have enabled them to help others and heal them keeps making their lives difficult.

They'll not be able to enjoy life like others because crowded places would keep making them feel vulnerable. They'd keep feeling exhausted just by venturing out and may develop strong aversion from social gatherings and crowded places.

Many empaths may feel that their nature of getting overwhelmed anytime without provocation is a big problem. They may think that the lack of control is a nuisance, and they have no power to control it. However, that depends on the perspective of the empath and his/her preparation to deal with it.

Identification Is Important

The first step towards solving any problem is its identification. The way our society functions in general, most issues are easily brushed under the carpet. It is common for people to advise others with severe psychological problems to laugh it off or try to remain more engaged, and everything will get alright.

People categorize all obese people as voracious eaters and begin advising them to have control over their diet. They firmly believe that a lack of control over the desire to eat can be the only reason behind weight gain. They do not even consider factors like genetic makeup, comorbidities, depression, and other such factors.

It is a natural desire to overlook problems or undervalue them. However, shying away from the problem doesn't solve them. On the contrary, it can escalate it.

People know very little of empaths. The people who do not belong to the class of empaths but have comparatively higher sensitivities would like to have the title of being an empath. Popular fiction has created an air of mystery and power around empaths that makes the traits sound desirable. However, actual empaths are dealing with real problems. They have to struggle with emotions and sensitivities. They are not at the luxury of thinking about the fancy title of being an empath.

You must understand that being an empath is not a problem. But, not dealing with the issues that come along with it can be. Everyone who feels for the challenges of others isn't an empath. Understanding the problems of others is empathy, where you try to invoke the pain of others within yourself. There you try to imagine what others might be feeling. An empath is a person who feels that pain and emotions of others from within.

Some highly sensitive people might also be able to feel the pain and emotions of others. They are also very sensitive to light and sound. They have an aversion to large groups or crowded places. They may also have a deep desire to help others and would be able to feel their pain.

But empaths go even further than that. Empaths can also feel subtle energy. An empath may be able to experience the feelings and emotions of even those life forms that are unable to express themselves. An empath has the power to internalize the pain and emotions of others instantly. These are some distinguishing traits that only empaths have.

The world may always find it challenging to identify and understand an empath. But, an empath needs to have a correct assessment of the self. That is a must for the betterment of the empath as well as society.

CHAPTER 6
Who Is An Empath?

An empath is an ordinary individual with an open spirit. Defining all empaths in a single statement is impossible because empaths are of various kinds. However, the most common trait among all empaths is their high sensitivity. All empaths are highly sensitive individuals.

Empaths are individuals with the unique ability to feel subtle energy around them. These highly sensitive individuals can absorb the emotions, feelings, and pain of others around them. They act as sponges for feelings and emotions.

These are the qualities or traits common among empaths. But, it isn't an exhaustive list. Empaths can be of different kinds. Some empaths may easily absorb the physical symptoms of people around them, while others may act as sponges of emotions and feelings. Some empaths have intuitive abilities, while others may possess telepathic powers. From feeling the needs of the plants and vegetation around them to healing others, there are a lot of things that empaths can do.

However, before all this, an empath must have the realization of these powers and control over the vulnerabilities.

Much before any other kind of division, you can divide empaths into two broad categories:
1. Awakened Empaths
2. Unawakened Empaths

You might have heard about the things empaths can do, and they all look splendid. These stories have found elaborate space in popular pop-culture. Most of these programs portray empaths as telepaths, psychics, and fortune-tellers. These programs are putting false impressions on the mind of the unsuspecting audience. They make the fact believable that all empaths possess these powers and very well know how to use them. Nothing can be farther from the truth.

Awakened Empaths

These are the individuals who have realized that they are different and that they possess a gift. Much before anything else, it is a must that an individual identifies the self. An awakened empath is an individual who acknowledges who he or she is. An awakened individual will not be perplexed at the rush of emotions felt all of a sudden without a provocation. An awakened empath would know the extent of powers possessed, as well as the limitations that come along with them.

These individuals are not unaware or unsure about themselves. They realize the things they can do and those they can't.

Being an empath is a gift, but it can only be so if one realizes it. Awakened empaths are those that know it and are always conscious about it.

They are the individuals who have a clear idea of their abilities, and they are continually working on honing them. Possessing an ability would mean nothing if the individual has no consciousness of it and never works on improving it. It is like a capable painter working as a car mechanic. Painting is a creative work, and repairing requires one to be methodical; it won't work well for that individual.

Clear identification of the ability and constant endeavor to enhance those abilities is the mark of an awakened empath.

The most important part of being an awakened empath is faith in the abilities possessed. The world can always doubt your skills as it doesn't see what an empath can see. However, an empath must never doubt those abilities, and then only they'll work. Unwavering faith in what you perceive to be your strength will make you an awakened empath.

Awakened empaths have the power to make a difference in the lives of people around them. They are the ones who know their abilities, trust them, and continually work to enhance them.

Such empaths have the charisma to stand out in the crowd. They are confident and can function smoothly in most conditions.

A skill most common in empaths is the ability to get an accurate first impression of a person they meet. Awakened empaths can usually assess the true nature of the people they meet more accurately than others. Their ability to sense the subtle energy and vibes behind the visual façade is responsible for that. They also possess powerful, intuitive skills.

In a nutshell, awakened empaths are confident and skilled individuals with the power to look deep inside the people they meet. They know their strengths and weaknesses, and hence they don't easily get overwhelmed by the emotions they feel.

Unawakened Empaths

As you could easily guess, unawakened empaths are the stark opposites of awakened empaths. They might possess similar abilities as awakened empaths. Still, because they neither realize their skills nor have control over them, they keep feeling crushed under the weight of those very abilities.

An awakened empath is like a person with a car driving uphill. Although he/she has to go up against gravity, the vehicle would help the empath go up. The system helps in the whole process. There is nothing to act against. Now imagine an awakened empath on that same road with a vehicle without the fuel. The task would become immensely tricky because the same car that was supposed to help would act as a piece of extra baggage.

The burden of carrying high sensitivities and powers is what makes the lives of unawaked empaths so challenging. They have a gift, but because they do not know of it, that gift becomes a burden.

Ordinary people fancy the powers they believe an empath has. Won't you feel lucky if you were in a position to know the real intent of a person in front of you in the first meeting itself? Won't that make business deals and negotiations so much easier?

That would be a bargain for most people in the world.

Imagine how wonderful it would be if you could sense the coming danger beforehand. We all want to have that reliable power of intuition that can warn us of all the bad things about to happen. Empaths have that power inbuilt. Yet, it'd make the life of an unawakened empath difficult as that individual would have no way to use that information or to trust it.

Being an empath is a gift. However, not realizing that you are an empath or not having control over your faculties can quickly turn into a curse.

CHAPTER 7
The Struggles Of Living As An Unawakened Empath

I have remained focused on the fact that unawaked empaths may have to lead a miserable life, and they'd find no way out of it. The reason for emphasizing this fact is significant. However small the exclusive group of empaths may look, when you look at the number in absolute terms, you won't be able to ignore it.

The empaths are not more than 1 to 2 percent of the total population. Although this looks like a very insignificant percentage, when you look at it in absolute terms, hundreds of millions of people across the globe fall under this category.

Such a large percentage of the population with a confused and vulnerable state of feelings and emotions isn't good news. The problem doesn't just end there. If the people with a sensitive, emotional state fell straight into one category, it would have been straightforward. However, that's not the case.

The percentage of highly sensitive people in the world is around 15 to 20 percent. It means a much bigger class of people are there with a somewhat resembling state of mind but without the abilities.

It becomes very easy for others as well as for the victims themselves to consider themselves as just being emotionally vulnerable. However, they go far beyond being emotionally vulnerable. They are not only prone to get emotionally hurt very quickly, but they also act as emotional sponges. It means they'd keep absorbing the pain and suffering of others and may not understand the way to deal with the surge of emotions.

They'd keep having intuitions, premonitions, weird dreams, and psychic sightings but wouldn't know what to make of it. In such a scenario, these very powers can turn into nightmares for the victims.

An unawakened empath may keep living a miserable life as that individual would be lifting the weight of emotional, psychological, and sometimes even physical pain of people around. That person would also remain crushed under the influence of abilities that are beyond his/her control.

From early childhood, empaths begin experiencing these powers. In the beginning, it isn't that difficult as people don't call you mad for behaving differently or talking things that may sound nonsense to them. But, as you advance in age, your experiences remain the same, but the rest of the world begins to think that you haven't grown.

It is a reason most unawakened empaths experience confusion, anxiety, and inability to regulate their emotions. They are never able to adjust to others. They feel exhausted in crowds but are never able to identify the real cause.

Empaths, awakened or unawakened, can feel negative energies. However, unawakened empaths are never able to ascertain what to make out of that feeling. As a result, they are unable to distance themselves from those negative energies and end up being miserable.

One of the biggest problems is their inability to manage their energy fields. Empaths are porous, and they act like sponges when it comes to absorbing feelings and emotions of others around them. Awakened empaths understand this crucial fact, and the most important thing they learn is to differentiate between an emotion that originated within them and the one that doesn't belong to them. In this way, they can prevent unwanted emotional overload and also help the people in need.

Whereas, an unawakened empath wouldn't be able to carry out this crucial differentiation and hence remain crushed under the burden of those emotions.

Unawakened empaths usually suffer from a lack of confidence. The power of intuition is the biggest asset of empaths. Awakened empaths know they can rely on their intuition as they have faith in their capabilities. Unawakened empaths lack this confidence, and hence they are always dangling between logic and intuition. Self-doubt and confusion become a permanent feature in their lives.

They are afraid of groups but long for friendships and love. This longing can also become a problem for them because their desire for love makes them rely on others too much. They become easy targets for exploitation, and narcissistic people take full advantage of this.

They remain trapped in their web of assumptions while the world is never in sync with them.

Being an Empath Isn't a Choice

Being an empath isn't a choice that you get. It may run in your genes and hence keeps getting passed on as a legacy—some people empaths in many different circumstances, like after having near-death experiences or severe accidents. But, it is never by choice that you get to become an empath.

However, it is always in your control to determine what you make of your abilities.

You can keep living the life of an unawakened empath and remain a subject of personal ridicule. Unawakened empaths have weak personal boundaries, and hence they always remain vulnerable to absorbing feelings and emotions of others.

The most dangerous aspect of these problems is to give in to addictions and other methods to become numb to such influx.

It is common for empaths to feel overwhelmed with emotions, feel hurt, uncomfortable, emotionally unsafe, shy, anxious, exhausted, and drained. Self-pity, over criticism and self-criticism, too many rejections, fears, and other similar feelings may lead to insomnia and guilt. All these feelings can easily lead to the development of escapist tendencies.

The easy way to escape is to numb your senses or lower your sense of perception, and overdependence on alcohol, drugs, and gambling always looks attractive and comfortable options. Some people who do not go to such lengths try to find refuge in other things like food, shopping, or other such habits.

Empaths must understand that taking refuge in these addictions is an easy way out but a temporary recourse. It may cut you off from your problems momentarily, but they'd always be there.

The path to becoming an awakened empath may look tough in the beginning to some empaths, but it is the best way in the current scenario. For an unawakened empath to lead a satisfying life full of joy and normalcy, there is not a lot you'll need to do. Even if you begin acknowledging and accepting yourself as an empath, you'll find it much easier to live with your gift.

The sooner you develop the realization, the faster the doors to timely identification of feelings and emotions would begin. These are the most significant troubles in the lives of empaths. They keep getting bombarded by unsolicited emotions. They are unable to identify them and hence remain troubled.

Part of the process of turning into an awakened empath is to learn to differentiate. It will help if you learn to distinguish between your emotions and the emotions of others. Once the identification is clear, emotions coming from outside will not have a toll on your mental balance.

Another step is to get the fear of being an empath out of your mind. Empaths keep struggling with the emotional turmoil for a significant part of their lives. When they begin getting any help, they want to get rid of it. But, being an empath isn't a choice. You can't shake it off. It would be best if you learned to live with it.

Finding True Love Can Become Tricky

It is natural for all of us to desire love. The need for love and attention is even more significant in empaths. These individuals absorb more pain and suffering from their surroundings. Loved ones around them can help them in healing and provide positive energy. However, empaths may find it very difficult to get true love.

Being an empath is very tough, and living with one isn't something different than a roller-coaster ride. Empaths can easily get overwhelmed by the emotions and energies of the people around them. It can make them fearful of intimacy. They'd long for more and more along time, and this can bring a rift between relationships if the other partner fails to understand it. An awakened empath will know this need and discuss it with the partner to create a balance. However, unawakened empaths are unaware of this and hence end up in strained relationships.

All empaths have a natural ability to feel and absorb the emotions and feelings of others, and their partners are no exception. Here, it is essential to note that they are not discussing the emotions and feelings but absorbing them directly. Personal boundaries get trampled very easily. Unawakened empaths are never able to enforce these boundaries and find themselves in a fix.

Empaths feel more overwhelmed by emotions and need more alone time than others. Struggles with anxieties and depression are everyday affairs. They may get upset over tiny things and not know the reason for that, and such things can be tricky to understand for their partners.

All these things make the love lives of empaths increasingly tough. However, that doesn't end the need to have someone to love, and this is the weakness most often exploited by narcissists.

Narcissistic people often identify an empath's dependency and people-pleasing behavior and use it to their advantage. They keep playing with the vulnerabilities of empaths.

Unawakened empaths especially need to remain aware of toxic relationships as they are prone to fall into their trap. These relationships can become a significant emotional drain on them, and they may find themselves in deep trouble.

CHAPTER 8
Unraveling The Nature Of An Empath

As I have also mentioned earlier, it can be challenging to put empaths in a single rigid frame. All empaths may not show the same signs or all the signs and traits, and hence defining the true nature of an empath in a single frame isn't possible.

There are several signs and traits that empaths exhibit, and only an empath can understand whether he/she possesses them or not.

If you search on the internet, you can easily find hundreds of signs and traits of empaths. However, even ordinary people can find a number of those traits within themselves on some self-introspection.

Not only this, but several personality tests on the internet can also term you as an empath.

Do those sound believable? Yes.

Are they correct? In 99% cases, No.

You must understand that empaths aren't mutants, and hence if you broaden the traits or soften them up a tad bit more, a considerable number of people would get included in that category.

Most people who aren't empaths and do not have those struggles that empaths face are mesmerized by the powers possessed by empaths as portrayed in TV programs. This fascination makes them want to believe that they also possess those traits but never have realized them. The innate desire to have those powers and feel special makes them think so.

Now, there are several characteristics like a desire to spend time in nature, easy to manipulate, free-spirited, hates injustice, and other such things can't be defining traits.

Most of us living in concrete jungles like to spend time in nature. Even for the most conservative of the individuals, it'd be hard to digest the fact that they aren't free-spirited, and none of us would like to believe that we love injustice. At least on a personal scale, we all love justice.

These can not be the defining traits of an empath because they are very general.

There will be some traits that are not very general, and yet even they may not be very accurate because even **Hyper Sensitive People (HSP)** would also have those traits.

For instance, a defining trait of empaths is that they are highly sensitive individuals, but so are HSPs. As far as being sensitive is concerned, empaths and HSPs can be equally responsive to feelings and emotions. The real difference lies in the qualities beyond that. HSPs are sensitive to sensory-stimulating signals like light, sound, and temperature. They may feel exhausted at crowded places and like to live alone.

HSPs are sensitive to feelings and emotions but may be unable to process them further. An empath may go much beyond merely feeling those emotions; it absorbs them. The company of a grieving individual will not only make an empath sad like an HSV, but the empath may also experience that same loss within.

Feeling the pain and emotions of people around them is a gift empaths share with HSPs. However, they have the additional ability to feel energy. They can absorb and internalize subtle energies emanating from the people or environment around them.

Defining Characteristic Traits of Empaths

Highly Sensitive

It is the bone of contention. It has been an issue that has created the highest amount of confusion. There is no measure of sensitivity, and it is subjective, like pain and pleasure.

Simply being sensitive wouldn't make a person an empath. Anyone can be shy, introverted, and vulnerable to feelings and emotions.

Empaths take sensitivity to another level. Being sensitive not only means getting affected by the environment around, but it also means to read even the slightest difference in it. An empath would also be able to sense the façade of faces people wear quickly. They have the innate ability to feel the pain and emotions of the people around them. It means, when an empath is around you, words may not be needed to express your sorrow or discomfort to the empath. An empath would be able to feel it within himself/herself.

The sensitivities are physical, emotional, as well as spiritual. An empath may also be able to feel the presence of various kinds of energies around them.

Very Sharp Instincts

Empaths have very sharp instincts. It is something that empaths possess with distinction. Empaths have a very keen sense of intuition, and it is something that can be a boon as well as a curse.

The power of intuition is a widely debated subject.

It might have happened with you several times that you knew what was coming. There are times when, before making a decision, your instinct is telling you to do something else. You go with your logic, and in the end, the result is terrible.

We all have this gut feeling, and we all are troubled by it because it is mostly directing you against logic. It leads to self-doubt, confusion, and anxiety.

Now think of a person who is getting these intuitive thoughts more strongly and all the time. Awakened empaths know that they can trust these thoughts, and their life becomes somewhat easy. However, most unawakened empaths are never able to trust their intuition, and hence they keep feeling the confusion and anxiety.

The power of intuition is an asset that an empath has. Most people have this power of intuition, but it is neither too specific nor reliable enough. An awakened empath would have high confidence over this power of intuition and would be able to do much with it.

Unawakened empaths would also have this power of intuition, but they'll neither be able to trust these signals nor act against them. It will create a lot of confusion and doubt.

It is a distinguishing trait of an empath. Empaths don't just have ordinary intuitions like the rest of the people around them, but their intuitions are deep and defined.

Ability to Absorb Emotions and Feelings

It is another distinguishing characteristic trait that most empaths possess. An empath can easily absorb the feelings and emotions of other people around them. They don't need to talk or with those individuals. It can happen even by looking at pictures or videos.

Now, this can be a very damaging quality to have. Imagine you are having a great time at a diner with someone special. Someone you have been longing to meet. Everything has been going great, and all of a sudden, someone with deep wounds passes by. You'd feel that pain and sorrow within you. The joy and exuberance would evaporate, and sadness would engulf you.

It isn't a hypothetical situation but a reality of the life of most empaths. Enjoying life in public can be very difficult for them because there can be no control over the feelings, emotions, and energies that you may encounter.

Can you recall any such incident happening with you?

Empaths will have a long list of such incidents where they felt deep sorrow within themselves without any provocation. Everything would have been going perfect, and they'll suddenly feel overwhelmed by the surge of contrasting emotions.

It is a reality most empaths have to learn to deal with in their personal lives.

The surge of emotions that they absorb is generally so strong that it becomes challenging to distinguish whether the feelings are their own or of someone else.

The problem is so significant because it is happening all the time. We can't live in a box. We are social beings, and meeting and interacting with others is a need. It is also the most significant cause of discomfort.

Aversion from Crowded Places

It is a point that would need several qualifiers. Introverts hate crowded places as they don't like to interact with others. HSPs don't want to go to crowded places as such places make them feel drained. Many people, in general, have a dislike for overcrowded places. Does that qualify all those as empaths?

You can't use the disliking of crowded places as a characteristic feature. Empaths don't like overcrowded places because they feel overwhelmed by the surge of emotions they begin absorbing.

Empaths are generally introverts, but many empaths aren't. Being an introvert isn't the real cause for their aversion to crowded places. The emotional overload that they experience at those places is the real culprit. At crowded places, the empaths get bombarded by a variety of feelings and emotions possessed by people around them. They begin acting as magnets. It isn't the fault of the crowd but their inability to keep such emotions away.

Even the extrovert empaths who enjoy the company of others can begin feeling exhausted in the crowds because it isn't their external demeanor that's getting challenged but the internal emotion processing mechanism.

Fear Intimate Relationships But Long for Love

It may sound paradoxical for many people, but this is a reality of life for empaths. Empaths deeply desire love. Empaths continually get bombarded by emotions from all sides, and this does cause a lot of damage. They become emotionally vulnerable. Love is a magical potion that can help them heal. If there is someone whom they can trust and rely upon, it becomes easier for them to recover.

However, most of the time, they are not able to sustain their relationships.

Empaths want love, companionship, togetherness, but they also need their me-time to recuperate. When they find someone who loves them, they usually begin getting smothered by love and don't get the breathing space they need.

Most people are unable to understand their exact need for love as well as some alone time.

If the person they love is too possessive, overpowering, or demanding, empaths will begin feeling suffocated.

It is the reason failed relationships can quickly become a regular feature in the lives of empaths. Ordinary people usually never get to see this aspect of their lives when they aspire to become empaths or have their powers.

Empaths Long for the Me-Time

As we have already discussed in the previous point, the me-time is a must for empaths. It is the time needed to recover from all the pain and suffering they might have experienced.

Awakened or unawakened, being an empath is never going to be easy. An empath is bound to experience emotional pain and suffering that others might never know. Their experience of such emotions is going to be very wide. Personal pain doesn't mire their lives. They are always suffering from the pain of others.

Getting over such pain would always need a lot of effort. It is the reason they need alone time. It can't be done in the company of others because then the constant absorption of energy would keep taking place.

The alone time is very soothing for empaths. It isn't the time they are getting bored or missing something but getting healed from within.

It is a thing that distinguishes the need for alone time in empaths from others. They are not trying to run away from the world like introverts when they seek seclusion, but they are just healing internally.

Empaths are Soft Targets for Energy Vampires

It is a hard reality of the lives of empaths that they always need to be cautious of energy vampires. They can never be too careless in scrutinizing people around them.

If you carefully look around yourself, you'll find several toxic people around you that may be a drain on your energy. These are energy vampires.

Energy vampires are the people around who feel entitled. They don't take accountability for anything and may hold others responsible for everything that's going wrong.

Empaths are easy targets for energy vampires.

In the regular course of life, everyone gets attacked by toxic people who act as energy vampires. However, most people can easily avoid such influences. Various kinds of vampires, like narcissists and rageaholics, can have a profound impact on the mental and emotional balance of empaths.

People with narcissistic attitudes are challenging to deal with most people, but they can be big trouble for empaths as they are emotionally vulnerable.

Such energy vampires are easily able to overpower the empaths emotionally. They can make the empaths feel worthless and incapable of being loved. Self-pity and gloom can begin taking over the heart of an empath, causing further damage and pushing the empaths towards addictions.

Greenery and Nature is Replenishing for Empaths

It is also a frequently misinterpreted characteristic. Most people living in the concrete jungles love greenery and the lap of nature, as it is a refreshing change. However, it isn't the same for empaths. They need natural surroundings to heal themselves.

Human beings are different. We all have different emotional makeup and personal boundaries. Most of the time, the exchange of feelings and emotions is also one-sided. It means, while an empath may be able to absorb the emotions and feelings of others, there is no way to transfer them elsewhere, and hence the empath has to live with that burden.

While it is easy to absorb emotion due to the porous nature of the self, it isn't possible to transfer them to other individuals with the same ease.

However, that's not the case with plants and nature. Nature is simple. It is absorbing and forgiving. Empaths find it very easy to pass on their burden of emotions and feelings to the plants and other natural objects silently, and it is very healing.

It is a reason empaths love nature so much and need to go in natural surroundings very often to replenish themselves.

One shouldn't get confused between nature lovers and empaths.

Weak Personal Boundaries

One of the most significant weaknesses of empaths is their inability to have boundaries. No matter what kind of an empath a person is, having firm personal boundaries is not a trait to be found.

Most people would feel the sting of watching a car crash victim. But, an empath may feel crushed. Most people wouldn't mind walking past a homeless person begging on the streets. If an ordinary person's heart weeps, he/she will give some money to the beggar and walk past. If possible, an empath would certainly give money, but even after that, wouldn't be able to forget the pain the beggar has been feeling long after leaving the scene.

Weak personal boundaries are a substantial reason empaths have poor relationships. Empaths can look into the heart and mind of the person they love, and they keep doing that without respecting the boundaries. It eliminates dialogue from the relationships and brings encroachment. It can crush relationships.

Empaths find it very hard to say 'no' to anyone. This tendency can lead to overexploitation, which most empaths suffer.

Empaths have Very Strong Senses

It is a natural trait that most empaths share with HSPs. Both have powerful senses of smell and taste. HSPs are introverts, but empaths can also be very talkative. Their ability to listen is also very sharp, and some may also be able to see much better than others. The ability to view better has less to do with the quality of vision but more with objectivity. They have a sharp eye, and they miss very little even when they are just looking at things with a cursory eye.

These are some of the traits that are common in empaths. However, this list is by no means exhaustive as empaths are of various kinds. A telepathic empath will have profound communication abilities. Dream empaths will be able to remember their dreams well and then deduce meaning from them.

Like everything else, being an empath also comes with its positives and negatives. It is up to the empath to make good of them or keep rotting in them.

Being an empath isn't something straightforward. You get a gift and also a responsibility to hone that gift, or that same gift can become a headache for you.

Empaths are Very Generous and Mostly Unable to Say 'No'

Being generous is a quality most people like to have in them of the people around them. But, empaths take generosity to the next level.
They have a people-pleasing attitude, and they try to go to any extent to make people around them happy. It is a trait that makes them susceptible to exploitation. Some people understand their desire to be the savior and begin exploiting them.
Empaths generally find it very hard to say no to anyone. Many people take advantage of this weakness, and empaths still keep serving.

CHAPTER 9
What Does It Mean To Be An Empath?

Being an empath isn't something you can shake off. If you are an empath, then every area in your life will get affected by it. You can't expect to have the good things of being an empath and leave out the bad ones. If being an empath gives you the ability to know about the feelings and emotions of loved ones, you will also need to remain prepared to get bombarded by feelings and emotions of the people you encounter on the roads and your workplace. It won't be a choice.

Being an empath has a profound impact on every area of life. From your health to your love-life and work, being an empath affects everything. You can't expect to have an ordinary life like regular people. You will have your unique challenges and opportunities that you'll need to learn to handle.

Health

Health of an empath gets the hardest impact. You can be an empath of any type. Your abilities as an empath may empower your dreams, your intuition, your telepathic skills, or something else. As you can see, most of these abilities have to do with your mind. However, that doesn't mean that they won't affect your physical, emotional, or mental health.

Being an empath makes you a receptive person. Awakened empaths have more definite personal boundaries, and therefore, they get less affected by energies around them, and unawakened empaths have weaker limits, and they get affected more. But, they all get influenced, nonetheless. The only difference being, awakened empaths have more definite personal boundaries, and hence they can manage the influences better and are better in overcoming the challenges.

Even awakened empaths can't prevent the absorption of feelings, emotions, and energies. Just that, they are better at distinguishing the emotions and feelings that belong to them and the ones that don't. At the same time, unawakened empaths find it increasingly difficult to manage the constant bombardment of emotions and feelings as they can't differentiate between theirs and others.

It also has a profound impact on an empath's work life and outside interactions. Irrespective of your state of consciousness, venturing out would remain tricky. You are bound to get bombarded by a string of emotions and feelings when in crowded places. It will make you feel exhausted and drained. It is a sort of occupational hazard as it comes with being an empath. It would help if you learned to deal with it properly.

Environments with very high sensory stimulation also don't work well for empaths. For instance, an empath may not find dance clubs with loud music very attractive. There will be too much noise and physical touch involved. It can leave them overstimulated. As an empath, you must keep in mind to avoid such places as much as possible.

Physical contact of any form must be strictly avoided as far as possible by all kinds of empaths. It doesn't mean that you can't shake hands with others or hug your loved ones. It merely means that shaking hands with people you don't know shouldn't become a thing for you. It may be a norm for others and socially accepted greeting, but it can be an energy drain for an empath. While you may feel energized by shaking hands or hugging someone you love and appreciate, shaking hands or hugging someone you don't know might suck up your energy. Finding alternate ways to greet people would be better for empaths. They can greet people with folded hands as done in eastern cultures or bow down a little.

If you are an emotional empath, then it will be natural to get affected even profoundly as your body would be more receptive to emotions, feelings, and energies. You'd need more practice in distinguishing between various emotions getting absorbed. As an emotional empath, it'd be impossible for you to prevent the absorption of energies; however, if you can increase your interaction with people having positive vibes, you can benefit from them. As an empath, you are going to absorb energy nonetheless. Let it be a positive energy in the equal proportions that you get, and it will make healing much more manageable.

Being a physical empath isn't going to be any easier. A physical empath can pick the physical pain and suffering of the people around them. It means if you are around someone having skin rashes, you can expect to get some yourself. It calls for extra caution. However, there is also an upside to it. If you come in contact with healthy individuals full of positive energies, you may even get a part of that and thrive on it. It is a miraculous power.

Although it is easier to prescribe mixing with a select group of people, we all know that it isn't possible for all extent and purposes. We will meet all sorts of people and will be able to exercise limited control. Hence, it would help if you remained more vigilant about your mental state.

Low energy levels, anxieties, sadness, and mild stress are some of the milder symptoms to depict a toll on your health. If you are continually living in a negative or not in a conducive environment, you might get these symptoms without any remarkable or apparent cause. It should work as a signal that you need to make some immediate changes in your company, or you need to beef us your boundaries.

If you do not pay attention to these, they can result in severe anxieties, depression, and rage.

Staying for too long in a charged atmosphere is never advised for an empath as it can be very imposing on the personality of the empath.

Staying at the top of the physical, mental, and emotional state is a must for an empath because they are bound to carry some extra burden at the end of the day. If they begin the day under a lot of stress, it can seriously impede their performance.

Because being an empath isn't a disease, there is no medicine for it. However, there are ways to enhance personal boundaries and prevent invading emotions from affecting your mental and emotional health.

A healthy diet with a lot of green vegetables and fruits will provide you the energy and stamina to ward of the usual stress. You must also practice meditation daily as that can help you in stabilizing your mind and your heart even in the most aggravating circumstances.

If you are feeling overwhelmed by emotions and do not feel like taking extra burden, you must recuse yourself and stay in solitude or the lap of nature until you heal completely.

Empaths must deal with their health issues, in general, very promptly. Ignoring these issues can have a long-term impact on physical, mental, and emotional health, and recovery may be tenuous and tedious, if at all possible.

Love, Relationships, and Sexual Life

These are essential concerns of life, and an empath may struggle in all of them if they do not deal with them appropriately. We all long for true love and stable relationships in life. They help us become better people. However, we all know the outcome of fake love and toxic relationships. Even an emotionally stable person would find it very hard to get out of a toxic relationship. The more harmful they are, the harder it becomes to get away from them. It can be an ordeal for an empath who will undoubtedly have greater appeal for people who are dependent on them or need them. They have the innate desire to act as a savior, and that thinking can be disastrous for them.

Due to the importance of all three aspects, we'll discuss them one by one.

Love: Love is the magical potion that can heal the aching heart of an empath. An empath is always longing for love as it is getting filled with pain, sorrow, hatred, and other such dark emotions of people around. The company of a loved one can help an empath energize and heal. An empath will feel much better in the company of someone he/she enjoys being with and trusts completely.

However, while an empath's heart is always aching for the company of someone he/she loves, too much intimacy can become overkill. Empaths want to be loved, but they also want their alone time. Usually, the people who love you are too much concerned about you, and they invade your space unknowingly; this can cause real trouble.

Although it may not be a problem for an awakened empath who understands this need and discusses it openly with the loved ones, the unawakened empaths usually get caught in the fix. They aren't even aware of the need, and that can lead to misunderstandings, mistrusts, and loss of love.

It is a must that an empath understands the unique circumstances he/she is in and discusses it with the loved ones before any rift arises. Being open, direct, yet considerate is the only solution to find a middle ground. Although this is an ideal solution, most empaths would find it very difficult to arrive at it.

Empaths may also feel emotionally spent most of the time, and hence they might not be able to contribute a lot. It can make the other person feel odd. However, empaths would have to communicate this to their loved ones and explain the way things are in their lives. Chances are once they understand, love would flourish easily. The complication lies in the level of communication and understanding. Most empaths can understand the needs and feelings of others without the use of words. They can remain in the delusion that even others can do the same and hence not use words to communicate their situation correctly. It is the reason for most miscommunication.

Relationships: Nobody throws an open invitation to narcissists like empaths. It is in their nature to feel drawn towards people in need of love and support. Narcissists are damaged people who like to suck up all the positive energy in the person trying to support them, and the empaths may even feel that. Still, they'd find it increasingly difficult to distance themselves from selfish or narcissistic people. Narcissists give them a sense of purpose as they know they are needed a lot there.

It is the reason, empaths who have such a robust, intuitive self feel impulsively drawn towards narcissists and toxic relationships. Such relationships rapidly become abusive, and empaths know that they are getting exploited. However, they are not able to resist the temptation of another try.

Empaths have an innate desire to help the people in need, and they need to understand that there is a limit to what they can do. They cannot keep on suffering at the hands of their tormentors and keep going back.

Relationships can act as an elixir in the lives of empaths. A healthy relationship with a good-hearted individual can help empaths function with great ease and confidence. On the other hand, a narcissist can continually make them feel inferior and inadequate. They'd keep getting hurt inside out and wouldn't get time to heal their hearts.

Empaths would need to understand the importance of relationships in their lives and the roles they can play. They'd need to be extra careful while building relationships and not compromise on the critical aspects of finding correct people for relationships.

Sex: It is an aspect that's generally not discussed much. However, ignoring sex can be a big mistake. Empaths treat sex in a very different way than ordinary people. For empaths, sex is a medium to release the pressure built inside them and not just a way to express their love to the partner.

It is where the rift begins.

While most people want sex to be a beautiful expression of love, the way empaths treat sex and indulge in the act; it looks as if they are using the sexual act for physical gratification. It is leaning more on the side of lust and less on the emotional side of it.

Most of the time, their sexual partners are not able to understand this distinction, and they begin to feel like an object of sexual gratification. The usual instinct is to deprive empaths of sex, and that can lead to frustration, emotional outbursts, and further rifts.

The things are not as they may seem to the partners of empaths. An empath will usually not engage in a sexual relationship with an individual whom he/she doesn't love. One must understand that love is the basis of that sexual act. However, empaths may not be able to portray that accurately while they engage in sexual activity.

It is the responsibility of the empaths to explain their need for sexual release and its importance for them. Even after that, their partners may not be able to provide them comparable sexual gratification, but as long as there is proper communication, things can work smoothly.

Work

Work is the third most crucial front an empath needs to deal with in life. Crowded places or places filled with charged people can be challenging for empaths. However, this may not be a choice for empaths working in highly competitive environments. When an empath has to work at places where there is a lot of excitement, rush, stress, or other such excitable feelings floating in the air, they end up soaking the emotions of a lot of people and hoard them in the form of stress, anxiety, and panic.

Such a thing can affect their performance to a great extent as well as their behavior at the workplace.

Avoiding charged atmospheres or crowded workplaces may not be possible for empaths, but they can still learn to maintain some distance. Empaths need to understand that they can't keep absorbing emotions and energies and still perform at their best. They will have to make suitable adjustments.

It is always best to avoid heated debates in offices and try to find as much alone time as possible. The longer you can work on your desk all alone, the easier it would be for you to get over the absorbed energies.

You can also keep some plants and natural things on your workstation that can help in passing on the emotions and energies.

Regular meditation can play a fantastic role in keeping you centered and grounded even after staying in charged atmospheres for long. If you practice meditation regularly, you'll be able to enforce firm boundaries around you and also distinguish between the emotions and feelings that are yours and the ones you've absorbed from your surroundings.

Addictions

Until now, we have been discussing important things for a fruitful life of empaths. We have discussed the main areas of life that concern them the most.

Unfortunately, all empaths are not so fortunate to overcome all the issues. Their energy management is weak, and they do not get the release they need. Such empaths may also repeatedly fail in relationships and get exploited by narcissists and dominator energy vampires.

Such empaths find an easy way out in addictions. Alcohol, drugs, gambling, and sex is the usual way to numb the sensations and find some peace.

It is a path on which empaths find the ease and release they have been looking for all their lives.

They want the constant bombardment of emotions to stop, and that can't happen until they are in an inebriated state. It begins as an excuse and quickly becomes an addiction that they would find extremely difficult to leave.

The chemicals consumed may help in the intoxication of the mind and numbing of the senses but don't solve the problems causing them. The relief is momentary and false. Giving in to addictions is like trying to find brightness at the end of a dead tunnel.

Alcohol, drugs, and gambling are just some mediums that usually get most of the bad press. However, they are not the only addictions.

Many empaths begin finding solace in food and get addicted to food. They aren't eating food to fill their tummies but to absorb their pain and divert their attention from their current problems. Comfort foods, high sugar foods like desserts, especially become their favorite as high sugar content leads to serotonin release in the brain that makes us feel good.

Some empaths try to find solace and joy in shopping. As long as they remain immersed in shopping, they can divert their attention from the current issues. However, we all know that this trick doesn't work well in the long-term.

The sense of solace, joy, and fulfillment can never come for an empath from such addictions. These can only act as temporary diversions.

Instead, these addictions can open the floodgates of sorrowful existence, severe anxiety, and depression.

Trying to find a way through these addictions can be as harmful as self-medicating yourself while suffering from a terminal illness. The medication will not only lead to further pain and suffering, but you'll also live always in fear of something terrible happening in the end.

The best way out is to seek help. The best way out for an empath is to talk to someone you trust or take professional advice. There should be no shame in seeking help because, as an empath, you have immense potential, but that can be getting washed down the drain due to poor management.

Addictive behavior is destructive in its own right and harmful for everyone, in general. Getting out of addictions can be particularly tricky for empaths due to their impulsive nature.

However, if they engage in more productive ways to channelize their energies through mediums like exercise and meditation, they can get much better results. Meditation is a fantastic way to center your mind and lives. It helps in grounding, and you'll be able to manage your faculties better.

Getting out of unhealthy addictions should be a priority for any empath because it is only going to drag you deeper into the much from where extraction may become nearly impossible.

Psychic Abilities

In the end, we come to the topic that may have the interest of all the people who want to have powers like empaths. The empaths have to live a life ridden with deep fissures, and no one can accurately understand their pain in the real sense.

For all the trouble they have to go through and all the positivity, love, and compassion for which they are a medium, nature endows them with several powers that ordinary people can only desire.

One of the most common abilities in empaths is their power of intuition. Everyone has some intuitive capability, but in ordinary people, this power of intuition is very subdued.

They may be able to feel things about to come but have no reason to rely on that information, and there is never really any confirmation. Most of the time, what they think as their intuition is just a flight or fight response originating in a gut inspiring them to take the escape route. However, that's not the case with empaths.

The intuitive ability in empaths is generally highly pronounced. Although this power of intuition may keep the unawakened empaths confused, the awakened empaths know for sure that they can completely trust their intuition.

Now it may only seem like an added asset to an outsider, but most people would be willing to swap a lot to have such power of intuition. Imagine the kind of dangers you can dodge if you could even have a real clue about them. Empaths get this power by default.

This ability is just not limited to having some wild hunches, but many empaths also can see events far off in the future. They may have it as premonitions. It is a miracle, but if you have faith in your powers and the heart set in the right place, your consciousness can get connected to the collective consciousness of all the other beings and make such visions possible.

Some empaths can heal others not only emotionally and mentally but also physically. It is a power that can make you the most wanted person in your circle. Although it comes at the high cost of your health and well being, yet it is a power that can help people in certain specialized professions in assessing and understanding the ailments suffered by others more accurately. The ability to absorb wounds and illnesses and provide healing is a truth and not a mere hoax.

Some empaths can have vivid dreams that can unlock the secrets of past and future events. Some empath dreamers can accurately decipher the sleep-visions of others and explain their meanings.

Some empaths can sense energies around them and successfully interact with them. It might sound absurd to many, but for them, even the whole idea of empaths may look silly. Nevertheless, it is a possibility for some empaths. Not only this, but some empaths can also communicate with energies on the other side and ghosts.

Some empaths can easily read the minds of people in front. Some empaths don't even need words or a medium to communicate as they can connect telepathically.

These are all possibilities that become a reality for an empath, but they have a cost. An empath can neither ask for them, and most empaths don't even desire them.

These abilities are within empaths, but they do need to work on them and sharpen the skills.

An empath must understand that being an empath is neither a gift nor a curse. It is a condition with which most empaths are born with and have to learn to handle.

Once you have the gift, there is no turning back. Either you can learn to utilize it to its full potential and make the lives of others better and benefit from the satisfaction it gives, or you can keep sulking over your woes of being an empath.

Irrespective of the ability an empath gets, it is the responsibility of an empath to help others. That's something for which the heart of an empath always bleeds. Most unawakened empaths remain ignorant of such urges within them and keep ignoring them. However, whether you recognize the gift you have or not, it is going to be there.

If you are prudent enough to realize that gift, you'll be making your own as well as the lives of others easy. Some empaths do not recognize their powers and responsibilities and fall prey to their vulnerabilities or take the destructive path.

CHAPTER 10
Do You Think You Are An Empath?

It is a fact that the correct identification of an empath is difficult. There are scores of personality tests available on the internet that may identify most people as empaths. They fail to differentiate between people having empathy and real empaths.

Even ordinary people have empathy. It is in human nature to have empathy and compassion towards others. That doesn't make a person an empath.

It creates another problem that most people undermine. Due to this incorrect identification and no proper way to identify a real empath, most empaths are unable to realize their unique nature, abilities, responsibilities, and the requirements to recognize their gift.

The utter confusion, self-pity, and helplessness that ensues make the life of empaths pitiful.

As we have already discussed this plenty of times in this book, being an empath isn't a problem, a curse, or a disease. However, not realizing that you are an empath can lead to miseries.

An unawakened empath will have to live trapped under the burden of being an empath. That individual will have no other option than to bear the indiscriminate and unsolicited bombardment of emotions and feelings and won't even have firm boundaries. Realization is the first step towards course correction, and hence it is imperative that you accurately identify whether you possess the traits of an empath or not.

While trying to assess whether they are an empath or not, most people make a crucial mistake. They try to look in the wrong direction. They are mostly looking for the abilities empaths possess. If that is the path you were going to take, you are bound to be disappointed.

It'd be better if you understand that an unawakened empath will most likely possess all the problems an empath faces and least likely to have any of the abilities.

The reason is simple. You don't need practice to exhibit weaknesses while you need to practice a lot to master a skill. Training can't help you in acquiring any power that empaths possess, but it'll help you in enhancing those abilities.

It is also essential to understand that even at the height of being a fully awakened empath, you are not going to have the famed powers of spiderman, superman, or any other cartoon character that wears underwear over pants.

Jokes apart, empathic abilities help you in enhancing your sensory or cognitive powers to a level not possible for ordinary beings.

The simple purpose of this chapter is to make you understand whether you have the underlying symptoms of an empath. If you feel that you own several systems of an empath, it will help you know the cause of the problems experienced, here onwards, you can begin working on them.

There are some straightforward questions that you need to ask yourself and come up with an honest answer. Try to be as critical as possible in those answers. You must understand that the correct reply to those questions can help you in getting out of the mental and emotional trap that you might feel caught up in at the moment.

It would help if you answered these questions without an expectation of a gain or the fear of a loss.

Do you think you are incredibly moody and suffer from depression or anxiety?

An empath can have a cacophony of emotions inside, while everything on the outside may seem to be perfect. Everyone else can use noise cancellation headphones to cancel out the loud noises and focus on the objective. Empaths can find no way to do so with the constant bombardment of emotions happening inside. All this can make their moods volatile.

Most empaths don't even get to know the source of emotions and feelings they are having at that moment. Now, think of yourself in that position. Being in a perfectly pleasant setting and enjoying time with your loved ones and all of a sudden, gloom overshadow your mind. It strikes you like lightning, and you can't even tell why it has engulfed you. Has that ever happened with you?

Such emotional explosions are everyday occurrences for empaths because they can absorb emotions from people around them. Not only this, but they can also feel the emotions with the same intensity as the characters in the movie or program might have felt if it was a reality.

Have you ever felt like an emotional sponge?

When an individual has to go through such a string of emotions on a day to day basis, the development of anxiety and depression is usual.

Have you ever felt anxious about the sudden changes in mood or emotions while in the company of some loved one?

In such situations, you begin to feel as if you are losing complete control over the situation. There is a looming fear that things might go out of your hand anytime. Unless they already haven't gone out of control.

All this can lead to severe anxieties and depression in unawakened empaths. It can be too much to handle for the people who don't know the real cause of such emotional turbulence.

If you feel that you fit in this description, you have one qualification of an empath.

An empath can have a cacophony of emotions inside, while everything on the outside may seem to be perfect. Everyone else can use noise cancellation headphones to cancel out the loud noises and focus on the objective. Empaths can find no way to do so with the constant bombardment of emotions happening inside. All this can make their moods volatile.

Most empaths don't even get to know the source of emotions and feelings they are having at that moment. Now, think of yourself in that position. Being in a perfectly pleasant setting and enjoying time with your loved ones and all of a sudden, gloom overshadow your mind. It strikes you like lightning, and you can't even tell why it has engulfed you. Has that ever happened with you?

Such emotional explosions are everyday occurrences for empaths because they can absorb emotions from people around them. Not only this, but they can also feel the emotions with the same intensity as the characters in the movie or program might have felt if it was a reality.

Have you ever felt like an emotional sponge?

When an individual has to go through such a string of emotions on a day to day basis, the development of anxiety and depression is usual.

Have you ever felt anxious about the sudden changes in mood or emotions while in the company of some loved one?

In such situations, you begin to feel as if you are losing complete control over the situation. There is a looming fear that things might go out of your hand anytime. Unless they already haven't gone out of control.

All this can lead to severe anxieties and depression in unawakened empaths. It can be too much to handle for the people who don't know the real cause of such emotional turbulence.

If you feel that you fit in this description, you have one qualification of an empath.

Are your mood swings erratic and without the backing of a probable cause?

It is again just a question to confirm the previous point. Do you often have mood swings out of the blue?

Most people might find this question odd because the mood swings are, by default, out of the blue. However, even in that case, people do have a basis for mood swings. When they are upset, deep down, they know the thought that's troubling them. They have the backing of experience to support that emotion, and that experience is causing the pain.

In the case of empaths, there is no backing of the experience. The experience causing the mood swings would be missing in its entirety. There would be no probable cause for your sorrow. You are merely feeling sorrowful for the pain in the world.

If that is the case with you, you must pay attention to other symptoms as well.

Do you often feel like a misfit?

It is not an accurate description of an empath. I want to say categorically that empaths are not misfits.

However, you cannot deny the fact that until empaths discover their true identity and powers, most of them feel like misfits. They can't sit in groups, and they don't feel comfortable in crowds. They get emotionally overwhelmed on petty things and, most of the time, even without a cause. These many things are enough to brand them as misfits, but the list doesn't end here.

Empaths have a completely different outlook of things, and working for the self is not one of them. Their heart is always bleeding for others while they are themselves in a petty state. Even then, they are more concerned about others. It also makes them a fit case to be branded as misfits.

Do you feel like you are a misfit?

Have you ever thought that you look at things from a completely different perspective than others?

If that is the case, exploring deep may be useful for you.

Do you have a very low tolerance for heated arguments and yelling?

Empaths are highly sensitive beings. We have already discussed this in several forms, and yet we will again keep coming back to this topic as it has the essence.

Empaths, in general, have a very low tolerance to heated arguments, loud noises, and yelling. You will rarely find even an extrovert empath in such settings.

Empaths may have a view about things, but they'd generally keep it to themselves and certainly avoid getting into heated arguments. They have a very low tolerance to loud noises and yelling because when someone is screaming, the atmosphere gets charged with emotions, and it subsequently begins inflaming the feelings and emotions of the empath. Either it is an awakened empath or an unawakened empath, you'll find both trying to avoid heated arguments, debates, and people who engage in too much yelling and screaming. It is always an automatic decision.

Do you feel inclined to help others and care for them?

Again, there can be a lot of confusion with this point. I'd like to believe in the goodness of humanity, in general. I want to think that most people feel for fellow human beings, and the people who can ignore others in pain are few and far between.

While most people feel a sense of righteousness in helping the people in need, empaths may feel a compulsory obligation to do so. Their heart is always bleeding out for others. They may be ready to help others with complete disregard for their safety and capabilities.

The fact that they feel more deeply for the pain of other fellow beings even without being told about the problems is entirely their propriety.

Do you feel a compulsion to help others even when you know that it isn't going to be right for you?

Do you sense the pain and suffering of others and feel aggrieved?

If these emotions have been striking you left, right, and center, you can be an empath.

Do crowded places make you feel overwhelmed?

We have already discussed this point in some detail. It isn't uncommon for some people to feel overwhelmed in crowded places. However, the reason for being overwhelmed may differ in every case.

HSPs feel overwhelmed as they have high sensitivities to noise, smells, light, unwanted physical contact, and other such things. They want to get away from this discomfort at the earliest possible.

Introverts may want to avoid crowded places because they don't feel like they belong there.

However, empaths feel overwhelmed at crowded places because they are unable to control and absorb the surge of emotions they feel. In a crowded place, there would be people with no pain or sorrow. They would be radiating exuberance. It is something positive for an empath. But, at the same time, there would also be a lot of people with pain, sorrow, and sufferings entrenched deep within their hearts. An empath cannot have a filter not to absorb those emotions. It means at the same time; an empath may be getting positive and negative emotions. It can be confusing and terrifying altogether.

It is the reason most empaths feel overwhelmed in crowded places. Even if the site is not radiating mixed feelings and emotions and all the people are sad or happy simultaneously. Just think of the surge of that emotion an empath might feel because it is not the emotion of a single person but a collection.

Empaths try to avoid overcrowded places to prevent the sheer intensity of emotional assaults that happen at such sites. They are bound to feel overwhelmed with emotions if there are too many people around.

Have you ever felt that in your case?

Are crowded places too overwhelming for you?

Do you feel spent, exhausted, and drained after coming from crowded places even though you didn't interact with anyone?

Even as a child, have you always been very sensitive to the feelings and emotions of others?

It is understandable for people to become emotional as they grow because their sensitivities about pain, suffering, and emotions develop. However, as a child, our priorities are simple. As a child, up to a certain age, the survival of the self is the biggest priority.

As a child grows a little, personal happiness is the priority. A child is a happy being until a force is applied to make the child unhappy, or the child has to live in a miserable environment like extreme poverty, hunger, or terror. Even in those environments, kids find ways to entertain themselves and remain happy.

It is tough to make a child feel gloomy for very long.

However, even as a child, have you felt very sensitive to the feelings of others?

Has the pain and suffering of others besides your family members made you feel sad for very long even after it has been away from your sight?

Have you felt the 'happy' switch thrown off all of a sudden and begin to feel sad with no apparent reason?

As a child, have you experienced a switch of emotions as you might feel now?

If you answered in affirmation to these questions, you must undoubtedly probe further.

Does spending time in the lap of nature help you heal and make you feel rejuvenated?

Again, this is a contentious point, as we have discussed it earlier. Most people may feel better in the lap of nature because it is a refreshing change and provides a break from the monotony of ordinary life.

However, the reason for empaths to feel so is entirely different. The empaths do not need greenery, jungles, oceans, and hills to break the monotony, but these natural landscapes help them heal internally from the wounds of absorbing so many emotions.

Empaths absorb a lot of emotions in a day to day life and have no barriers around them. Awakened empaths can differentiate between their feelings and emotions and the ones that don't belong to them. Nevertheless, that can't prevent them from not being sad at the misery of others.

Unawakened empaths don't even have those filters. They get bombarded by a string of emotions continually and have no expertise in identification and separation. They keep feeling overwhelmed without having an experience attached to those emotions.

Now, while the empaths can absorb these emotions easily, it isn't easy to get rid of them. These feelings and emotions stick to them like leeches.

There is no medium to pass over these emotions easily. Nothing has the depth and simplicity of emotions to absorb them apart from nature.
It is a reason empaths love the lap of nature, jungles, mountains, creeks, riversides, and beaches so much. These aren't recreational places for an empath but a reservoir to submerge emotions long-held by them.
Do you feel light-hearted and healed after visiting such places?
Do you find it helpful to have lots of plants around you at your home or even at your workplace?
Do you feel a particular attachment to any specific plant?
If you answered in a yes, they might be helping you in offloading your emotions.

Have you always struggled with the idea of saying 'No' and failed miserably?

It can again be a contentious classification, but please bear with me. Many people might find it very hard to say no. However, it isn't what they say that matters but under what conditions they may say it.
Some people can't say no to others to avoid embarrassment. If you are among them, this doesn't make you an empath.
Some can't say no to their superiors, elders, parents, teachers, and bullies. The reason is fear or intimidation. They feel threatened by the consequences of replying in a 'no.' Even you can't classify such people as empaths.
However, some people can't say no because they feel that the people at the other end might get hurt or feel sad. They feel obliged to serve them and cater to their needs. They take it as their duty to cater to the needs of people in question and are ready to fulfill all the justified and unjustified demands in fear of harming them. Such people can be empaths getting exploited at the hands of narcissists and dominators or other kinds of energy vampires.
It is a fact that empaths usually have weak personal boundaries. Even the awakened empaths can fall into the traps of narcissists because they have an inherent need to cater to the needs of others and become the savior of someone in need. The narcissists are needy and opportunists that can make use of this weakness very artfully.
Have you ever felt that you have been getting exploited, and you were still unable to break free, although you knew that it was a toxic relationship? It happens very often with empaths because, by nature, they can't see others in pain.

Do you own the feelings and emotions of others as your own?

Many empaths can make a very poor distinction between their own emotions and the emotions they absorb from others. It becomes a cause of the massive emotional overload they bear most of the time.
Awakened empaths learn to differentiate between their own emotions and the emotions that come to them from outside. They can manage their mood and emotional health better.
However, many empaths and usually unawakened empaths are unable to do so. They keep treating all emotions as their own and have to suffer a lot.
Do you always know that the emotion or feelings you are having are your own, or is there confusion at times?

Do you want to be left alone?

Many people like to live alone. There are the loners, then there are introverts, and then there are hypersensitive people. All these want to be left alone as they feel tormented in crowds. However, you can classify none of them as being an empath.
All these people want to be left alone for different reasons.
The loners have an aversion to people they don't know very well. They can mix well with the people they like. They have no problem being with people who support them emotionally and by other means. They only want to stay distant from people who might challenge them or may pose a threat by any means.
The introverts are only trying to prevent opening up to anyone. Mixing with people would mean they'd need to disclose something, and they are most afraid of doing that. Some are not confident enough to speak as they fear ridicule or embarrassment. The rest of them only want to stay confined with themselves. Their reasons for limited outreach are simple.
Hypersensitive people or HSPs don't like to mix with a lot of people as they are sensitive to noise, arguments, getting hurt, and challenged. The more they mix with people, the higher would be the risk of sensory assault. It is the reason they like to keep to themselves and prefer being left alone.
Empaths, on the other hand, want to be alone so that they can overcome the emotional overload. Empaths are necessarily not loaners. They don't fear the company of others. On the contrary, they might prefer the company of particular individuals that can help them heal.
Empaths can soak energy, feelings, and emotions from people around them. While being in a crowd may mean indiscriminate bombardment of emotions, being in the company of known individuals with positive

energy would mean absorbing positive energy. There is no reason for empaths to fear that.

Still, empaths would need a lot of alone time to get over the emotional overload they might have experienced. They can use this alone time for sitting quietly, or they can also meditate for centering their mind and grounding their energies. The ultimate purpose of this alone time is to re-energize and heal.

Do you feel better after being left alone for a while regularly?

Are you able to shake off the heaviness of the emotional burden if left alone for a while?

If that was a yes, you certainly need to probe deeply.

Do sensory inputs overstimulate you?

It is a symptom that may be shared by empaths and HSPs. Both may have an aversion to light, sound, smell, and other sensory inputs that are more intense than usual.

Although you cannot treat it as a definitive symptom of an empath, it is undoubtedly a trait that all empaths exhibit.

Intense sensory inputs overstimulate the empaths.

Does sleeping early seem like a tough job?

It may be the case with many empaths, as they usually have insomnia. Many people are night owls these days. People like to work till late. Burning the midnight oil has become a fashion in the corporate culture.

Innovators, writers, and creators like to work in the calm of the night when there are minimum sensory inputs to break their focus.

However, all of these lose their sleep for reasons utterly different than empaths.

When an innovator or creator is awake at night, there is an idea taking form in mind. Their minds are busy and highly active. That's why they resist sleep.

An empath's mind, on the other hand, might be as calm as the sea. There might not be any thought on the visible surface. However, deep down, several emotions are depriving them of sleep.

If you feel perfectly calm and yet sleep seems to ditch you for very long every night, you may need to probe further.

Have you ever felt the presence of energies and spirits you?

Now we are entering the world of speculation. The speculation is not whether there are energies or spirits or not, but whether what you feel are spirits or not.

Our mind is a fantastic make-believe machine. If you begin thinking of the presence of an entity, the brain can make it possible in your perception.

The schizophrenics won't ever believe that their world is imaginary. Everything in their world is happening for them in reality. Therefore, we are not talking about make-believe realities. Instead, we are talking about experiential realities.

There are energies, and all empaths can feel them. Irrespective of their state of wakefulness, empaths can feel energies and vibes. Most empaths use this sense to form an impression of the people they meet. They don't judge people on their external demeanor, but by the vibes they generate. Some empaths have more reliable energy reception, and they can feel the vibes more strongly than others. In the same way, some empaths can feel spirits close to them.

I used the word speculation in the beginning because, as an unawakened empath, you may not have the experiential reality to differentiate between a spirit or powerful energy and your imagination.

Therefore, you'll have to rely solely on your senses and discretion.

Have you always felt eager to do everything to keep your relationships intact?

Empaths have high people-pleasing aspirations, especially for the people they love or admire. They want to do everything in their might to keep them happy and content. They won't hesitate even to get degraded to make their loved ones happy, and this makes them prone to toxic relationships.

Although it isn't an excellent thing to have, it can be a good thing to watch out for if you want to have a classifying feature of an empath.

These are some of the things that are most common among the empaths of all types. You can try to answer all these questions honestly, and if you feel that you can fit in the description of most points, you may need an in-depth assessment.

As mentioned before, being an empath isn't good or bad but a condition. You are a person with some specific abilities and weaknesses. If you have a clear assessment of your personality, you may be able to work on your weaknesses and strengths.

It is always beneficial not only for you but also for the people associated with you. Being an awakened empath, you can be of great help to others in the form of emotional support and healing. If you have specific abilities, you can utilize them to help yourself as well as others.

PART III
EXPLORING FURTHER- GOING DEEP

CHAPTER 11
All Empaths Aren't The Same- What Kind Of An Empath Are You?

There is a general misconception that being an empath would be the same experience for everyone. There can be nothing further from the truth.

It is a fact that fundamental realities may be similar for most empaths; every empath may have a different experiential reality.

Being identified as an empath is only a distinction that helps in understanding the basic perception levels of an individual. However, not only the abilities but the trials and tribulations of each empath may differ. Empaths can have different powers based on their strengths in various segments. An empath of one type won't necessarily have capabilities of only one variety. It can be a mixture of multiple senses; some may have their core-strengths based in one faculty, while others may possess one or more. An empath doesn't get to choose these.

Nature is the ultimate enabler, and an empath is only a medium.

Therefore, it can be challenging to describe all kinds of empaths as the variations can be many. However, for the sake of better understanding, we'll discuss some of the major categories of empaths.

If you go searching on the internet, you may find information about many more types of empaths. It'd be unfair to say that those kinds of empaths are not there, but knowing those many types is only going to add to the mental clutter and help in no way. Excessive information can only cause information overload and help by no means at all. Therefore, it is always better to stick to the basics while you are still scratching the surface.

Once you have developed a thorough understanding of the concept, you can freely explore them, and you'd only find that most of the types described as different classifications are just variations of the same categories. Seeing that after you have a grip on the subject always brings clarity, whereas absorbing that information without knowing that subject would lead to mental-muck.

There are three main categories of empaths.

No matter what people tell you, there are only three main categories of empaths. The rest of them are just sub-categories or poor spin-offs.

Emotional Empaths

These are the most common empaths. It is crucial to understand that empaths aren't very common. Only 1-2 percent of people fall into this category. It runs in the genes; hence, a very high number of empaths remain confined to specific geographical locations and families.

Therefore, one is not very likely to find empaths walking on the streets wearing their empath hats for easy identification.

They are rare and difficult to spot. Even with this rarity, a very high number of empaths never really acknowledge themselves as empaths. Hence, they may be walking the streets with ordinary people without knowledge about themselves.

It shrinks the group even further. Most of the power empaths have only become apparent when an empath has realized full potential. It means that an empath can live and die without having any effect or presence felt. The only power that is usually visible and is also a symptom of being an empath is the sensitive nature of the empaths and their ability to absorb the feelings and emotions of people around them. Most empaths experience this.

Within the limited group of empaths, emotional empaths are the highest in number. It is the reason people consider all empaths as readers of feelings and emotions. There is no logical base for this presumption.

The sheer number of emotional empaths dominating the scene is so high that they have become synonymous with the whole category.

Emotional empaths are highly sensitive to the emotions and feelings of the people around them. They may inadvertently soak the feelings and emotions of people they come across and experience those feelings within themselves.

It means that if there is an emotional empath in a joyous environment, he/she may enjoy life even with several hardships because there will be a continuous inflow of positive and harmonious energy.

At the same time, if there is an emotional empath at a place where there are people in grief and sorrow, that empath will also feel the pain and sorrow with the same intensity.

The emotional empaths can feel and experience the feelings and emotions of people around them.

It is a gift and also a curse simultaneously. It is a gift because such empaths will be able to share the pure joy of the loved ones. It can become a curse as those empaths may also have to experience the pain and sorrow of every individual crossing their paths.

They may be able to console their friends better as the same pan within them. However, they may also have to feel the pain of people they may meet but may not know. Hence, while they may feel their pain, they will not have the experiences to back the pain, and the cumulative pain they might have to bear can be immense.

Awakened emotional empaths know how to handle their emotions better as they learn to distinguish between the emotions originating within their self and the ones coming from others. Once they learn to do that, it becomes easier for them not only to handle the emotional burden better but also to help the individual suffering from the emotional pain as they have genuinely experienced their pain. There can be no better person to counsel such people and set them on the right path.

Most of the time, when people go to a psychiatrist, the doctor keeps reassuring you that he/she understands the pain of the patient. However, deep down in the heart, the patient knows that the doctor might understand the illness, but there is no way to feel that pain. However, that'd not be the case with an emotional empath. This empath would have felt that pain and would be able to help in healing it collectively.

Unawakened empaths may have it tough on them as they might find it difficult to bear all that emotional overload and pain without an experiential reality.

It is similar to banging your head in a wall. When you hit your head, there is pain. However, you exactly know the cause, and although you feel the pain, there is no fear of the unknown causing the pain.

Early identification of the signs, acknowledgment of the condition, and faith in your abilities, are the three steps towards emancipation.

For help in relieving the stress of emotional overload, you can practice meditation and also talk to someone you trust.

If there are still issues, you can make use of several problem-specific remedies discussed in the second part of this book.

Physical Empaths

It is the second most widely recognized category of empaths, also known as healers. Physical empaths have the gift of tapping into the physical energies of people around them. They can not only sense the physiological issues in people around them but even feel those issues within their bodies.

Physical empaths can be very helpful in feeling chronic illnesses that keep on simmering inside the body without any symptoms for years. They can experience energy blockages as well as imbalances inside the body.

Although this may look fanciful, being a physical empath doesn't come without its trials and tribulations. When a physical empath feels some problem, the empath is also absorbing or soaking a part of that problem and experiencing it. The empath would need to develop a mechanism to cleanse their body of the absorbed energies.

Physical empaths can be amazing healers and bring great insights if they are in the field of health care. Physical healers can make a lot of difference to the lives of people around them even if they aren't specifically in health care. They may touch lives in beautiful ways on a day to day basis.

However, they'd always need to remain cautious that too much exposure to crowds can cause exhaustion, and they may take more burden that they can carry.

A physical empath can easily absorb negative energy from the people he/she interacts with, and hence excessive exposure to them can be exhaustive. It can also hurt the health of the empath. At the same time, contact with healthy and radiating people will fill the empath with positive energy. If the empath can somehow maintain a balance, it'd work wonders.

Exercise, healthy food, and meditation can help a physical empath in radiating positive energy to more and more people.

Intuitive Empaths

The remaining types of empaths that you may have heard of belong with this category and the branches that follow.

It is vital to understand that the human mind has unlimited potential. All the other empath abilities that people have are related to the brain and its infinite power. Therefore, you can put them under one header for the ease of understanding.

An intuitive empath will have better clarity of thought and perception. Such an individual will be able to not only sense the feelings and emotions of a person but might also be able to understand that person with greater clarity. Such empaths have a clearer understanding of dreams and may also be able to perceive the dangers of the future much before they take place.

They may sense the energies and emotions of even plants and animals. Several animals can sense natural disasters much before they take place. Even the high-tech scientific instruments are not able to predict earthquakes and tsunamis as some animals can. In the same way, some empaths who are in tune with the earth can sense such dangers before they occur.

Intuitive empaths can have these sorts of mental abilities.

Some of the notable intuitive empath categories are:

Dream Empaths

Most of us dream almost every night, but very few people can remember those dreams. Whatever information people retain, they are unable to make out anything significant from those dreams.

That's not the limitation for dream empaths. They are avid dreamers, and they can not only have vivid dreams but may also be able to deduce useful and intuitive information from those dreams. Such empaths can also help other people in deciphering their dreams.

Dream empaths can get insightful cues from their dreams that can help in several meaningful ways.

These people can especially heal people carrying painful baggage from their past that has been making their lives challenging. They can help such individuals in understanding the meaning of their dreams and the things that they need to resolve to move ahead in their lives. It might look like the job of a shrink, but it is crucial to understand that a psychiatrist may have limitations of information that the individual may not be in a position to explain. A dream empath may not have such restrictions due to the intuitive abilities at disposal.

Precognitive Empaths

Most people understand precognition, as this is a term very commonly used in the movies. It might look like a part of the fiction, but some empaths may be able to see the future much before it happens.

There will be critics, but one must understand how energy works. We all have a consciousness that is just a part of the integrated awareness of this universe. At one level, everything has emerged from oneness. Therefore, our sense of awareness or subconscious can establish a connection with the larger consciousness.

Déjà vu is a phenomenon that sounds believable. Having intuition that you might have witnessed the events that happened just now much before is believable. Even ordinary people have had this experience several times. All this can only be possible if there is a force that can help us see those things.

Ordinary people have limited abilities to have such visions, while precognitive empaths can establish a much better link. It helps them see future events with greater clarity and consistency.

Telepathic Empaths

Telepathy is the ability to communicate with others intuitively and carry out an exchange of information. Many characters in popular TV programs owned such powers, and people felt fascinated by them. That was a time before the invention of mobile phone technology.

Nevertheless, even in this age, owning a power where you can penetrate the mind of someone else and know the real secrets can be invaluable.

Although telepathy doesn't work exactly like this, you get the framework. An empath having telepathic powers will be able to read the minds of others and connect with them intuitively.

Psychometric Empaths

These are the empaths who can receive some cue even from inanimate objects like jewelry, photographs, and personal possessions.

Some empaths can get the vibes of a person and also their emotional state from their personal belongings.

Mediumship Empaths

These empaths have a deeper connection with energies, and they can feel the presence of all kinds of energies around them.

No matter how much science tries to deny the presence of spirits, ghosts, and energies, it wouldn't change the fact that some people do feel the presence of these entities around them.

Those that can't understand their presence and motives might feel scared. Mediumship empaths have a deeper connection with energies, and hence they can communicate with and understand them better.

Such empaths act as the bridge between the spirits on the other side and this world.

Earth Empaths

These empaths have a deeper connection with the earth and all the changes happening inside it. They are in a better position to predict any sudden natural calamity or change.

These empaths feel deeply connected with the energies of the earth and therefore find it very easy to understand the changes in advance.

Plant Empaths

These empaths have a deep connection with their plants and may be able to understand their needs better. Such empaths can be very helpful for farmers as they can predict problems with crops and suggest ways to improve the harvest.

They may also be able to predict monsoon and drought more accurately.

Animal Empaths

These empaths can feel for the animals around them. They may be able to befriend animals easily and understand their needs. Such empaths can be very helpful in understanding their problems and provide a fitting solution based on their assessments.

CHAPTER 12
What Difference Does Being An Empath Have On Life?

The answer to this question will have two parts:
First, the impact of being an empath on you
Second, the impact of you being an empath for the world
We'll deal with both the aspects sequentially so that there is clarity on this question as it may arise in your life at several points.
Being an empath isn't an easy road. There would be many instances when you will have serious doubts about yourself, and you may want to believe that there is no such thing as an empath, or there is no merit in being so. An understanding of this question will help you in being determined on your path.

First, the impact of being an empath on you

It is the most important one of the two, and hence you must pay close attention.
Being an empath will always be a reality for you. It will never be a choice but a truth. Now there are two ways to deal with this reality.
First, you can acknowledge and accept the reality irrespective of the fact that you like it or not and begin working on modifying it as per your needs. It is always a better and more sensible way of dealing with reality.
Second, you may choose to live in denial for as long as you can wish or afford. It isn't a natural way, but many people still want to ignore reality and live in denial. They'll have to live with the consequences of being an unawakened empath. It means that they'll have weak boundaries or inferior filters to prevent getting affected by the oncoming emotions and feelings. They will not be able to distinguish between their feelings and emotions and the ones they absorb from the environment. They may suffer mood swings, depression, and severe anxieties, and these can worsen with time. They might experience all these and much more, but will not be able to experience the abilities that come along with them. They won't be able to develop the skills because they'd never acknowledge and accept their gift and have faith in it.
Most people are empaths by birth. It is just like having your limbs or other sensory organs, and there is no reason to run away from these.
Not recognizing that you are an empath can have a debilitating effect on your life as leading a healthy life may become very challenging. You may experience the rush of emotions that others don't.
However, it will always be up to you to recognize your gift and embrace it with the confidence and respect it deserves.

Second, the impact of you being an empath for the world

As an empath, you must understand that the world may benefit from your gift if you can polish it and use it for the benefit of others. You may get praise and lots of good wishes. You can do a lot of good to others by using your gift as we have discussed in the previous chapter the things empaths can do and the way those can make a difference to the world.

However, if you don't accept your gift or choose to ignore it, the world may never care. It will be more of an internal struggle for you, and the world can ridicule you for that but not sympathize.

Being an empath may not have been your decision, but it is a responsibility thrust upon you. We all come with specific responsibilities in this world. Some people succeed remarkably, and the world acknowledges, respects, and adores them. But, the unfortunate ones that are unable to fulfill their respective responsibilities are either ridiculed or forgotten without a mention.

It will always be up to you to make of the opportunity that has come in front of you.

CHAPTER 13
The Thin Line Of Being An Empath

We have discussed at length the potential an empath has. There is no doubt that if you are an unawakened empath, you will have an opportunity to become much more than you think you already are. There is a road that goes towards greatness or at least purposefulness. You can make your life more objective and goal-oriented, where you can reach out to more and more people and help them.

However, every path that goes towards greatness will also have a diversion at some point towards destructiveness.

Undoubtedly, empaths have a potential for greatness, but they also have an equal amount of potential for hara-kiri or self-destruction.

An empath who has such a great desire to serve others can quickly turn into a narcissist who would know nothing but to exploit.

Empaths and narcissists are two different personalities. However, they have a high affinity towards each other. If an empath doesn't get hold of the faculties and channelize them in the correct direction, the feeling of victimhood and entitlement may sweep in swiftly and silently.

An unawakened and immature empath may begin to undermine the need to earn and may start thinking that he/she deserves attention and the perks that come along.

If the thin line is blurred, then the tables might turn from the need to serve others to a sense of entitlement. It can be the first step towards narcissism.

The whole discourse for the empath may change from being independent, responsible, and self-reliant to dependency, getting served, and taken care of by others.

It doesn't take much of an effort to become a parasite from a benefactor.

With Great Power Comes Great Responsibility

These words from the movie spiderman hold great significance in the context of empaths.

You don't choose to become an empath. It is a selection made by nature. But because you are the chosen one, it is your responsibility to take it forward.

Even a beautiful rose comes with thorns. There is no success without challenges.

It is the responsibility of an empath to rise over brooding and make the best of the opportunities at hand.

CHAPTER 14
Beware Of The Things That Can Take You Down

An empath is a positive force. It is the reason an empath has to bear so many hardships. You are the beacon of positive energy who can redirect others in the right direction.

However, does that mean you won't face challenges? On the contrary, you may have to face many more hardships than the people you may guide.

In this world, the struggle between the good and the bad is eternal. The good can only win if it keeps reinforcing itself and doesn't allow weaknesses to penetrate its borders.

As an empath, it will be imperative for you to stay away from influences that can weaken you or subdued your powers. It isn't going to be easy anyway, but it'll become a lot harder if you give in to habits that are eroding in nature.

Your habits must help you in preserving your positive energy and keep your aura intact.

Emotionally, empaths can be under a lot of pressure most of the time. Giving way to emotional weaknesses can be very damaging.

An empath also needs to stay on guard all the time as negative energies are continually trying to take charge in various forms. They can come in the way of being too proud or looking for too much praise.

Therefore, it is the responsibility of an empath to adopt habits that keep detrimental influences away.

Preventing Negative Influence

Don't Try to Become a People Pleaser: When you are doing something beneficial for others, the desire to hear some praise is natural. Once in a while, you may get appreciation, and there will be times when you'll do what you do and move on without waiting for the praise. An empath should ideally function in this way. However, empaths are generally hungry for love and admiration. They do not care much about the ones that are usually grateful but desire the appreciation of the hard ones to please.

More often than not, the hard ones to please are narcissists that exploit this weakness of empaths. You'd keep trying to please them, and they'll keep exhausting you and draining you of the energy.

The empaths must believe in the true principles of 'Karma.' You only have the action in your hand, and the result should not be your concern. If you are deserving, you will get the result.

If you follow this principle in life, you will face less burden, and there will be much less emotional load on your heart.

You must understand that you do not have the responsibility to please a specific individual. Your reach can be extensive, and you must be useful for many rather than the ones you desire to please.

Do not Try to Carry People Over Your Shoulders: There is a beautiful quote,

> Give a man a fish, and you feed him for a day.
> Teach a man to fish, and you feed him for a lifetime.

It is a priceless lesson empaths need to learn. Many empaths begin trying to carry others over their shoulders. The people they are bearing become parasites as they understand that as long as they don't do anything, you'll fend for them.

It is going to drain you of your positive energy, and you'll begin losing the steam. You neither need to bear others nor need to ignore their misdeeds. The more you allow people to exploit you, the heavier they'll get.

Stop Being a Sacrificial Lamb for Others: Sacrificial attitude is a common occurrence in empaths. They'd not hesitate to take the blame of others onto their heads. Even when they know that they haven't committed a mistake, they may take the responsibility to save others. It may seem as if they have made a moral high ground, but they are digging a pit for themselves as well as for the people they were trying to save.

When they take the blame for the mistakes committed by others, they are effectively sending a message that there is always a way to escape after doing anything wrong. Crime and punishment should be proportional. When they don't get punished, they can become even more irresponsible. Even the empaths won't go unscathed.

If they keep owning the mistakes of others so rampantly, the burden they might have to carry can get crushing.

Using Victimhood as a Tool: This isn't something that most empaths do, but the ones that try to become a messiah of others may want to play this card. Once in a while, you can feel like a victim. However, you can't keep playing the victim card for too long. Once you get addicted to the sympathies and attention you get being a victim, you'd find it very difficult to get on your feet.

Most empaths have the ultimate desire for love and attention. The victimhood card may help them get both very easily, and they might feel compelled to play that card all too long, which can be dangerous. It can get them out of sync of their energies.

Permitting Others to Take You for Granted: Being forgiving is a virtue that most people don't possess. It is a rarity. However, you can't be so forgiving that people begin treating you as a punching bag or a doormat.

Getting trampled too often is a weakness and not a virtue.

An empath may have just one desire that is to serve others and cater to the needs of the ones that need their attention. However, this also has the potential to become a weakness very quickly.

You may have the desire to serve at the core of your heart, but you can't allow that to become a 'Kick Me' sign on your back.

An empath must develop the diligence to understand when someone is taking undue advantage of him/her because it may happen very often.

Not Conserving Your Energy: Energy will always remain a crucial issue. An empath can optimally function only when there is abundant energy. Empaths can begin losing power quickly. Several things may make an empath feel the emotional, mental, or physical drain.

If you allow your energies to get wasted on petty and useless things and people, you may not be able to pay attention to the real needy. If you are not able to help a needy, that will put an additional load of guilt on you. You must ensure that you aren't wasting your energy on useless people and objectives.

You must choose your priorities judiciously and remain clear of your objectives.

Preventing Emotional Burnout

In this world, nothing is endless. You can exhaust anything if you get on to it. Many empaths like to live in the sweet misconception that they have infinite love and affection to give. Little do they know that their ability to deliver is limited even more.

Emotional, physical, and mental burnout is the usual malice that affects empaths. Irrespective of the cognitive development and firm boundaries, it isn't possible to prevent total burnout. Empaths are sensitive beings, and they can't help but absorb the pain and suffering of others. There's nothing much they can do about it anyway.

However, it can be dreadful if an empath consciously begins attracting that drain upon himself or herself for long. The inability to say no to others and inadequate understanding of the limits is a common cause of the problem.

No matter the cause, if there is an emotional burnout, not only the empath but also the people around them would suffer.

There are several ways an empath can prevent the burnout:

Find the Healing Time: Every empath needs time to heal. It is the crucial me-time that empaths can utilize to ward off the excessive emotions and re-energize. At times, the empaths become so addicted to the appreciation and adoration they are getting that they stop paying attention to the emotional overload that can cause burnout.

Catering to the needs of others is a fantastic feat, but an empath must find alone time now and then to heal internally. Excessive load can affect an empath's ability to reach out to others through the energy field.

Decrease Attachment Dependency: Empaths are prone to attachments. They may keep denying the fact, but they want to cling on to the select few they love and adore. It can easily lead to dependencies that can hamper emotional and spiritual development.

They may become focused only on a few people and stop paying attention to the larger goals. It can also make them even more sensitive as their emotional focus would remain centered around a select few, and they would begin regulating the emotions authoritatively.

All this would eventually cause emotional burnout. More often than not, such relationships become toxic, and the empath begins to get dominated.

If an empath wants to prevent this, becoming dependent on a select few for all your emotional needs can be dangerous. An empath must try to find an alternate way to release pressure and heal. Meditation, exercise, and work can be the other areas that can also help an empath gain more emotional liberation.

Boundaries: Ineffective personal boundaries are the definitive cause of emotional burnouts in empaths. It is a widely recognized fact. The weaker the own boundaries an empath has, the poor will be the regulation of emotions that affect the empath from outside.

An empath must have firm boundaries to prevent excessive and overreaching assault on his/her emotional capacity.

Many a time, empaths give unhindered access to themselves to others. They become the oasis from which people can draw out anything anytime. There can be no way to sustain this behavior.

An empath must understand the limitations and also maintain a breather space.

An empath must also understand that there is a significant difference in feeling with someone and feeling for someone. One cannot own the emotions of others indiscriminately and survive unhindered.

Your heart may reach out for others, but you must set limits to the extent you can go. If you begin feeling for everyone around you, your system will be unable to hold it.

Effective boundaries are a must for the smooth functioning of an empath.

Try to Become Impersonal: It is the nature of an empath to begin to feel as others are feeling. However, empaths must understand that there is an extent to which they can keep doing so effectively.

If you begin feeling rage, apathy, hatred, and other such feelings within you, it won't take long for you to feel exhausted.

You will have to learn to become impersonal. While you can understand the emotions of people around you much better than anyone else, it'd be immature to begin to feel all the feelings within yourself. It can lead to emotional burnout very quickly.

Get Out of Savior Mode: This is another major issue that becomes a cause of emotional burnouts. Empaths make it their mission to save the lost causes. They must understand that they can't rescue those that don't want to in the state they are. They are likely even to drag you in their world as they act as swamps. The harder you try, the deeper you get.

As an empath, it isn't your duty to save the world. You can become a medium to help others through your skills, but you should drop the idea of trying to rescue the lost causes.

You must understand that they are eventually going to get submerged in their acts, and you are going to get repentance that will lead to emotional burnout.

Preventing emotional burnout is a must for an empath because if that begins to happen often, the empath may start to get drawn towards addictions to heal the pain and numb the sensations. It is a destruction path for any empath, and most walk down this road because they overestimate their abilities and then try to over utilize them.

An empath must respect the limits and always try to prevent negative influences on the personality and emotional burnouts as they can cause irreparable damage in the long run.

CHAPTER 15
Learning To Be An Empath With Confidence

No matter what you are, it is crucial to embrace it fully with confidence if you want to get anywhere. Being an empath can be no exception. There can be absolutely no doubt that the road to realizing your powers can be a bit bumpy.

An empath may not have it easy as several impediments come from your self-doubt. It is comparatively easy to tackle practical challenges as they are open and direct. However, when you get challenged from within, the fight gets tough.

But, you must understand that you don't have a way out. Being an empath isn't a religion that you can renounce or which you can stop practicing; it is an attribute.

The faster you accept your realities, acknowledge the challenges in front, and develop faith in your abilities, the sooner you'll be able to get hold of your faculties and life.

Several practices can help an empath in strengthening positive attributes. It would help if you did not only work on reinforcing your positive attributes but also worked on effective protection strategies and grounding techniques.

Reinforcing Positive Attributes

Develop Faith: Here, the word faith implies 'trust and confidence.' You can be a believer of any religion, or may not believe in any. It is inconsequential for an empath. Being an empath has nothing much to do with religion. You can very well be a believer, an atheist, or an agnostic, and it may all be the same for you. The most important thing that would determine the outcome for you would be your faith in your abilities.

Most people live in utter disbelief of their abilities all their lives, and sure enough, the skills evade them mercilessly. You must have complete trust in your abilities to make them work. It is the leap of faith you would have to take.

The only way out for an empath is to have complete trust in the abilities and continually work on refining them. It is like sharpening the ax. The sharper the tool, the shorter it'll take to cut down the tree.

Try Emotional Detachment: I know we have discussed this term in the previous chapter, but believe me, this is the biggest entrapment for most empaths. The stronger the emotional attachment you have, the easier it'd take for someone else to flip the switch for you.

As an empath, you must understand that the higher the potential for going up, the stronger is the attraction to look down and quiver.

Try to be as emotionally independent as you can. There is no harm in having more robust relationships and love, as they are the must. The problem begins when empaths begin to rely on those relationships for all their needs and lose their identity.

Meditate: Nothing can be more helpful for an empath to meditate regularly. Meditation is the most refreshing act that an empath would experience. It helps in grounding the energies and also unloading the emotional baggage you have been carrying.

It doesn't take much to meditate. You can do it practically anywhere, anytime. However, it'd be best if empaths can have a fixed time to meditate every day as that helps them in recharging themselves once a day, at least. If you aren't very particular about anything, it is easy to miss it in the veil of excuses.

Practice Release Regularly: It is another must for empaths. They hoard all types of energies within them as they are walking sponges of energies, emotions, and feelings. These can weigh them down and have a toll not only on their personality but also on their functioning.

They should try to release as much energy as possible through activities like running, shouting, screaming, and high-intensity workouts. The more spent force they can release, the lighter they'll feel.

Practice Mindfulness: Being mindful is a way of life. It is a technique that helps you remain grounded in realities, and you can easily pull yourself back from the emotional and mental entrapments.

It is a straightforward technique of living in the moment and experiencing every phenomenon with complete immersion. It can prevent empaths from falling in the trap of emotions, feelings, and experiences that do not belong to them.

An empath can easily ward off anxieties, stress, and negative emotions by being mindful of the current situation. It is no magic. On the contrary, mindfulness can help us break the spell of imaginary struggles that we create, causing stress and anxieties.

It is a technique that helps us in identifying reality with greater clarity.

Grounding Techniques

It is common for empaths to lose their ground or begin feeling out of sync. It often happens when the empath feels a rush of emotions or gets overwhelmed. It can create a feeling of detachment, disillusionment, and loss of connection.

It might happen very often with an empath due to high sensitivities. The good news is that such things aren't permanent. You can quickly get over such feelings by grounding yourself.

Some Easy Grounding Techniques are:

Aligning Your Root Chakra: The root chakra or the base chakra, also known as the Mooladhara, helps us establish connections with the mother earth. It allows all the negative energies built up inside us to seep into the ground and facilitates fresh energy restoration.

You can practice root chakra meditations, and you'll find that grounding the senses would become very easy. Root chakra meditation also helps us in strengthening our energies and building determination. If you have been struggling with self-doubt and self-determination, this chakra meditation can be of immense help.

Tree Exercise: Trees are the best example of benevolence, forgiveness, and tolerance. They are stable, reliable, and determined. An empath can draw a lot of positive energy from a tree and also unload a lot of negative emotions. Hugging a tree can help you transfer all the negative energy that can pass on from the tree to the ground.

Even sitting under a big tree can help you feel grounded.

Drumming: Drumming loudly and passionately can also help you feel more grounded—the vibrations arising from drumming help in settling the dust of emotions within you. It enables you to feel at ease, and you'll find your stress melting away after a session.

Using Essential Oils: Essential oils are also helpful in calming your senses. They have a very soothing effect on the energy chakras and also help in rebalancing your chakras. There are several ways in which you can use essential oils. However, empaths may follow caution when dealing with specific essential oils as they can even make you more excitable and overwhelmed.

Healthy Diet: Our food has a powerful impact on our personality and the way we function. People relying too much on hot and spicy foods are more likely to have a fiery temperament and emotional makeup. An empath needs to be stable and must retain energy for long as there is constant energy loss. A diet that comprises of root vegetables, nuts, and other energy-rich foods can help an empath in remaining grounded.

These are just some of the methods that can help you in feeling grounded, and you'll be able to function as an empath better.

CONCLUSION

Thank you for making it through to the end of this book; let's hope it was informative and able to provide you with all of the tools you need to achieve your goals, whatever they may be.

The purpose of this book was to clear the air about empaths and deal with the popular myths and misconceptions about them. Empaths are not fictional characters but a reality. However, they can be completely different from what people popularly consider them to be.

The objective of this book was to explain what it means to be an empath, and the kind of struggles an empath has to undergo. There is not much clarity about the trials and tribulations of empaths as the world only likes to know the fascinating things.

This book has tried to explain the real lives of empaths and the things they need to do to realize their powers and feel connected to the mainstream.

It is a painful thing that an empath who has an immense potential may spend the whole life cursing the characteristics that are a gift. Many empaths not only perish in oblivion but have to bear a painful existence because they are never able to learn to live with their condition.

The popular fiction either finds interest in lionizing their image or belittling them. This book has tried to present a realistic representation of empaths and the things empaths need to understand to become a fruitful part of the mainstream world.

However, it is still solving half the problem. This book would help you in understanding the complexities of being an empath and various aspects of it.

You would have come to know by now that empaths have to bear a lot of pain and trauma. Their lives cannot be as simple as ordinary people. Therefore, empaths need healing and support regularly.

If they do not get healing, they can become a dumping ground of emotions.

The second part of this book would help you understand various ways to carry out Empath Healing.

It would give you a detailed account of all the healing strategies and how empaths can enforce their energy fields.

I hope that you will be able to gain full advantage of the information provided by this book.

Finally, if you enjoyed this book, please let me know your thoughts with a short review on Amazon. It means a lot, thank you!

DESCRIPTION

Learn to Identify the Signs That Can Unlock the Doors of Mystical Powers Within You

Have you ever felt that your intuition warned you better than others in specific scenarios?

Has it ever occurred that you felt you had seen an event happening much before it took place?

Have you had bad feelings about something wrong about to happen?

Have you felt that others don't understand you fully?

If you've had such doubts before and never had an answer to those, this book is your chance. **Read More**

Do you feel that you are emotionally very volatile and have severe mood swings?

Do you think you can feel the feelings and emotions of others better?

Do you feel like a misfit as others are unable to understand you?

Do you feel unloved and drawn to people that seem to be narcissists?

Do you have an aversion to sensory inputs like bright lights and loud noises?

Does venturing out in crowded places seem to drain and exhaust you?

Did you know if you exhibit some of these symptoms, you may be an empath?

Pop culture has portrayed empaths is a very incorrect light. They have lionized the characters to the extent that they seem to be unbelievable. It sounds as if they can't exist. But, did you know that almost 1-2 percent of people in this world are empaths?

Did you know that most empaths keep struggling with emotional overload all their lives?

Did you know empaths may begin feeling exhausted as soon as they pass through crowds?

Do you know being an empath looks like a curse to most empaths, and it is more likely to stay that way for them?

Did you know that an empath doesn't need to live like that because there are ways to get over all kinds of empath fatigue?

If you want to know the ways to get over empath fatigue and get healing, **Read More**

Being an empath is an opportunity that can enable you to help others and live a more fulfilling life. However, some empaths are never able to capitalize on the opportunity due to their ignorance about empath healing.

If you want to know the real truth about empaths and the possibilities they have, and the ways to address issues that might come on the way, **Read More**

In this Book, You Will Find:
- Comprehensive understanding of empaths
- Explanation of fear and enigma behind empaths
- Understand, whether it is a boon or a bane?
- Learn why most empaths are never able to realize their potential
- Disadvantages of being an unawakened empath
- The things you can accomplish being an awakened empath
- The things that you'd need to do
- The reason people easily exploit empaths
- Why empaths fail to have stable relationships despite their caring nature
- The struggles in the life of unawakened empaths
- Characteristic traits of an empath
- Signs to look for
- Things it means to be an empath
- Different kinds of empaths
- The ways to prevent degradation of power
- Steps to reinforce the power

And Much More....

www.ingramcontent.com/pod-product-compliance
Lightning Source LLC
Chambersburg PA
CBHW071508070526
44578CB00001B/475